THE SIMPLEST OF TRUTHS

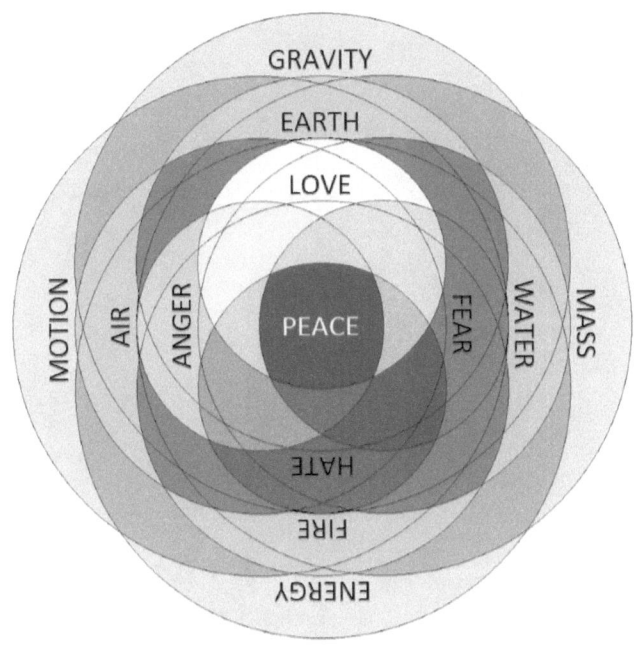

THE SIMPLEST OF TRUTHS

Our Earthly, Human, and Spiritual Ecology

GREGORY TUTT

2nd Edition

Copyright © 2018 Gregory Tutt.

All rights reserved.
No part of this publication may be reproduced, distributed, or transmitted in any form or by any means, including photocopying, recording, or other electronic or mechanical methods, without the prior written permission of the copyright holder, except in the case of brief quotations embodied in critical reviews and certain other noncommercial uses permitted by copyright law.
For permission requests, write to the publisher, addressed "Attention: Permissions Coordinator," at the address below.

Softcover ISBN: 978-1-64318-030-4
Hard Cover ISBN: 978-1-64318-035-9
eBook ISBN: 978-1-64318-036-6

Imperium Publishing
1097 N. 400th Rd
Baldwin City, KS, 66006

www.imperiumpublishing.com

THIS BOOK IS DEDICATED TO MY SON:
FROM ONE INTROVERT TO ANOTHER.

Contents

Introduction 9

Section 1 .... **12**
    The Four Cores 13
    Between the Two 18
    Eye of the Hurricane 23
    Walking out of the Dark: Part One 26

Section 2 .... **32**
    The Simplest of Truths 33
    Mass Transit 39
    Traffic 43
    Walking out of the Dark: Part Two 47

Section 3 .... **54**
    Our Spiritual Being 55
    The Heart of Community 60
    The Soul of Nature 67
    Walking out of the Dark: Part Three 71

Section 4 .... **77**
    The Peace Within 79
    Both Sides of the Coin 81
    The Conversation 85
    Walking out of the Dark: Part Four 96

Section 5 .... **107**
    Our Legacy 108

The Promise 113
Building Tomorrow.. 119
Walking out of the Dark: Part Five 127

Section 6 .... **147**
Whitewash.. 148
The King, the General, and the Priest 151
I Am Who Am 157
Walking out of the Dark: Part Six...................... 160

Section 7 .... **169**
God, Leadership, and Government 170
The Ring Governing 175
The Measured Democracy............................... 179
Walking out of the Dark: Part Seven 182

Section 8 .... **192**
Circles of Life 193
A Glance Back... 196
Clarify and Define.. 198
Torn: The Tear in the Fabric of My Soul 201

Introduction

***How do we live our lives today,
and how does that affect tomorrow?***

For me, writing this book became an exercise in defining my spirituality. As a guidebook, it is a journey of discovery on how you can come to understand your spirituality and how this influences all the relationships that surround you. The intent is to provide insight, that keeps you moving forward through mindfulness but also reminds you to stay grounded. Hopefully, it can aid you on how to become focused and be the best you can be at every point along the way.

Life is about relationships, and within every relationship, there is a unique exchange of energy. These exchanges—daily dialogues—should flow freely. The ongoing discussion within each relationship becomes, over time, an extended and more in-depth conversation, and these conversations are what starts the process of the discovery of each other. This process helps us to maintain the health of the relationships most important to us, or, at the very least, it can help us navigate a better path through life.

For each of us, our path to greater awareness of ourselves starts by understanding how our worldly experiences affect our emotions because our emotional state sets the tone for how we live our lives. This has a direct bearing on the level of success and fulfillment we will achieve, which in turn affects our quality of life. Our world pushes and pulls on us as individuals; it preys on our emotions. Without something to anchor our lives, we can be swept away on the currents of life and become lost. Our emotions bridge the gap between our physical self, the world we live in, and our spiritual self, which connects us to God—or, if you prefer, the conscious universe. Our goal is a peace-centered and balanced state of being.

Condensed down to the very basics, the higher awareness we have of ourselves in relation to others and even with the world around us stems from the spiritual gifts we receive from God. Yet, enlightenment does not start until we recognize those gifts and then apply them by embracing three truths: peace, equality, and the sanctity of life. This process begins with perceiving the peace hidden at the core of our being. Next, we must embrace equality for everyone and uphold the sanctity of their lives. These are our mandates on how we should strive to treat each other. Uncovering the peace at our core is not a simple matter; however, once revealed and then paired with the two mandates, these three truths together have the power to transform our lives, our religions, our politics, and our world.

In life, we should also define ourselves by two principles: integrity and wisdom. The two go hand in hand, without wisdom, integrity is fleeting, and without integrity, wisdom is hollow. For me, integrity and wisdom stem from the simplest of truths. However, integrity is defined by a commitment, to be honest, and fair in all of our relationships and transactions. It is then further refined and distinguished by measuring ourselves through our actions. We should always estimate the consequences of our words and deeds on others before we speak or commit those actions. Learning to do this can start us down the path to wisdom.

Wisdom, on the other hand, is merely perspective expanded. One may spend a lifetime in the shadow of the various mountains in one's life without ever exploring the horizons. Perspective is the art of viewing those mountains from different sides. Wisdom is the journey of discovery over and around those mountains. Yet wisdom comes not from conquering those mountains; it is acquired through every step we take to reach the summit and in the beauty that is revealed on the way down when our back is toward that mountain.

If I have a goal in mind for this book, it is that I want you to gain a higher level of awareness of yourself and the world around you. I hope that once you have finished the book, you want to reread it or go back and read parts of it again. I hope, too, that this book will spur a discussion that might start a dialogue with others or within a group and that the conversation will lead to new discoveries and, hopefully, a deeper understanding of each other.

Section 1

Inner Strength

Uncovering the peace within is not about finding an ancient or secret, all-powerful magic. Fully embracing the peace at our core helps us create inner calm, and this increases our inner strength. This strength bolsters our self-confidence and resolve, helping us to make better choices, regardless of the situation. Yet there is more to this than just being rooted in peace. Each of us also needs to embrace an attitude of equality and respect for those who are traveling with us in our moment in time. When fully realized, these three woven together can indeed be transformational. This is what is driving our cultural and spiritual evolution. These are the real gifts of God, and they give us the fortitude to live our lives with integrity and wisdom, to nurture and guide, and the ability to make changes in our lives and achieve a greater understanding of our world and ourselves.

The Four Cores

As individuals, we are capable of a wide range of emotions, but as described here, there are only four core emotions. Very broadly defined, they are *love, hate, anger,* and *fear.* If you envision them as four overlapping circles, then at the top is *love,* and opposite that is *hate.* These are our conscious emotions, our emotions of intellect and reasoning, and they drive our decision-making processes. From very early on, we learn to quantify and place a value on everything we experience and everyone that we interact with in our rapidly expanding world. Even as infants, we start building a library of people, things, and food, assigning a positive or negative value based on our experiences with them. Some of the ways our judging emotions of love/hate are expressed, is through our likes versus our dislikes, what is acceptable versus what is unacceptable to us, our respect toward others versus disrespect, and our trust versus mistrust.

Overlapping at the center and on either side of the first two are the circles of *anger* and *fear.* These are our unconscious emotions, instinctive and volatile, and they are what drive us to stand and fight or run away. They are our reactions to stressful situations, and we cannot always prevent them. As young children, we learn to cope with stress, but for most of our lives, we struggle to control and manage these two emotions. Some of the ways our reflex emotions of anger/fear are expressed, is through our aggressive versus tentative nature, reckless versus cautious behavior, a defiant versus submissive attitude, and insensitivity versus sensitivity.

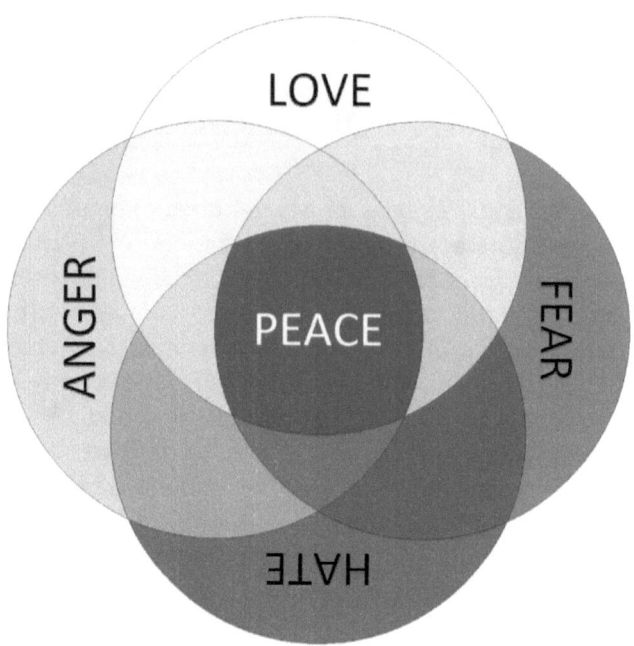

Generally, infants are born into this world with a parent or parents who are kind and loving. As their bodies and minds grow, and they transition from complete dependence to semi-independence, they learn some basic coping skills from their caregivers. Most infants and very young children gravitate toward love because they know and trust their parents, and it is the most comfortable place to be. Nevertheless, as infants and toddlers expand their horizons, they are exposed to more of the outside world and are faced with new challenges. As they do, they start to develop the first response emotions for coping with stress. Since the world pushes and pulls on their emotions, they eventually move away from pure love.

Everyone gravitates toward anger or fear at some point. How fast and how far depend on what challenges that individual has experienced and how he or she has learned to cope with them.

Over time, a default emotional response forms, but that does not mean we are permanently pinned to that one emotion. We still experience a wide range of emotions, but when our stress level rises, we will typically fall back on our default response emotion—usually with some measure of either anger or fear, whichever is the more dominant in our personality. The most unfortunate thing for any child is to be raised with very little love or kindness. Emotionally, these children can move beyond anger and fear into *hate* and live troubled and volatile lives. But with some help, time, and healing, it is undoubtedly within them to change their emotional state.

If you look at these four overlapping circles, you cannot help but notice the center. This area, where all four circles overlap, is significant to us. This is a null spot where our core emotions have no influence. Most people are oblivious to this, but everyone possesses this space. (The one partial exception to this is love, because there is more to love than our choice to like something or love someone. A different, more profound form of love stems from within that peaceful core and radiates outward.)

When we were conceived, our inner self, our soul, our individuality, and our life grew from out of that peaceful spot. At first, we were nurtured in our mother's womb, unaware of anything but this deep peace. When we are born into this world of chaos, we quickly forget that time of bliss. We begin to live our life in the whirlwind of emotions that spins around and shrouds our peaceful core. This is a state where love and hate can be as instinctive as anger and fear. That anger and fear can become as much of a conscious and driven choice as love and hate. This only highlights the fact that each emotion overlaps the other, and they all affect and influence each other.

This null spot, that deep peace that lies hidden within each one of us, is God. People will often say that "God is love," but God is more than just that: God is peace—the peace that surpasses all understanding. From within this inner peace God has given us love, but this is merely not enough to make a lasting difference in our lives. Only when we decide to embrace this inner peace and return that love can we experience any of the life-changing effects that God's peace and love offers.

With the knowledge that God as peace indeed dwells within each of us, we can all rediscover and experience this deep peace again. From within this peaceful core, God perceives all of our emotions but controls none of them. We are the master of our own feelings. Yet it is through our relationship with God's deeper form of love, and our decision to return that love, which can help us find ways to reduces the influence that the other three core emotions and the control they can have over us. This, in turn, helps us cope with an often cruel and unforgiving world.

This peaceful core, this null point, is not just empty space. There is more to it than merely nothingness; rather, it is a potent and overwhelming force which can have an impact on our lives. Through meditation and prayer, we can uncover that deep peace, and if we allow it, this peace can change or move our default emotional response to stress. As our anger/fear emotions move into a more balanced or controlled state, we naturally move closer to our peaceful core. When this happens, we start to realize that it is this state of calmness that quiets our instinctive emotions. Sure, anger and fear will still show up at times of great stress but, they should be far less intense.

It is harder, however, balancing the emotions of the intellect, which may not move until anger and fear are somewhat in balance or under control. Our feelings of love and hate are the quantifiers that we used to define ourselves within our world. It is not just about how we interact with it or how it relates to us but how we perceive it. This directly affects our attitude towards our world but also, how we relate to each other in general. Therefore, we must make very cerebral decisions and put aside our hate. With the help of this null point, that deep peace, we can make better choices that allow us to find balance and harmony in the world we live in and in our own lives.

God makes few demands on us, and recognizing this, there are only three truths we really need to embrace: God, in the form of peace, is the real core of your being; that your life, and every person's life, is sacred; and we are all equal in the eyes of God. After accepting these simplest of truths, your reasoning emotions may truly move. When we recognize that peace is the core of our being, and our default emotional response has moved into a comfort zone between peace/love and anger/fear, then we are in the best possible place to manage our emotions and ourselves. Moving forward, we can better navigate the world we live in, and the door is now open for us to do amazing things in our lives and in our society.

Between the Two

Our journey through life is based on how we as individuals perceive and interact with the world. We do this primarily through our emotions. Bring to mind the overlapping rings of our four core emotions, but now think of them in three dimensions. These four cores can be visualized as overlapping spheres aligned on a horizontal plane, and that null spot in the middle can be seen as a vertical cylinder. One end of this cylinder is planted in the world we live in, and the other is within the vastness of God. Now we can start to understand how we are rooted at both ends and exist between the two.

From here, we can grasp that our human nature is both worldly and spiritual. We are fixed between the two, held in the middle by the gravity of our world and the pull of God. We have been pulled from out of the world and made self-aware by the peace of God. Still bound to our world, we are set in motion by our own free will. Here we remain, suspended between the two until we slip from our earthly bonds and follow the cylinder that is our peaceful core, up into the vastness of God. Each of us is but one whirlwind of energy and emotion tethered between the two planes, one among billions of fragile tendrils reaching up from our world to God.

As living beings, we exchange energy with each other and our world. This energy is cyclic and cannot be retained. It ebbs and flows through our days and our lifetimes. Earthly energy seems chaotic but always follows a natural course, which we call the laws of nature. We live and work, drawing up this energy from our environment and each other and then expending it back into the world. Because we have an intimate connection to this energy, we can better grasp and understand this relationship and its dynamics, but since it is wild in nature, it is never entirely within our control.

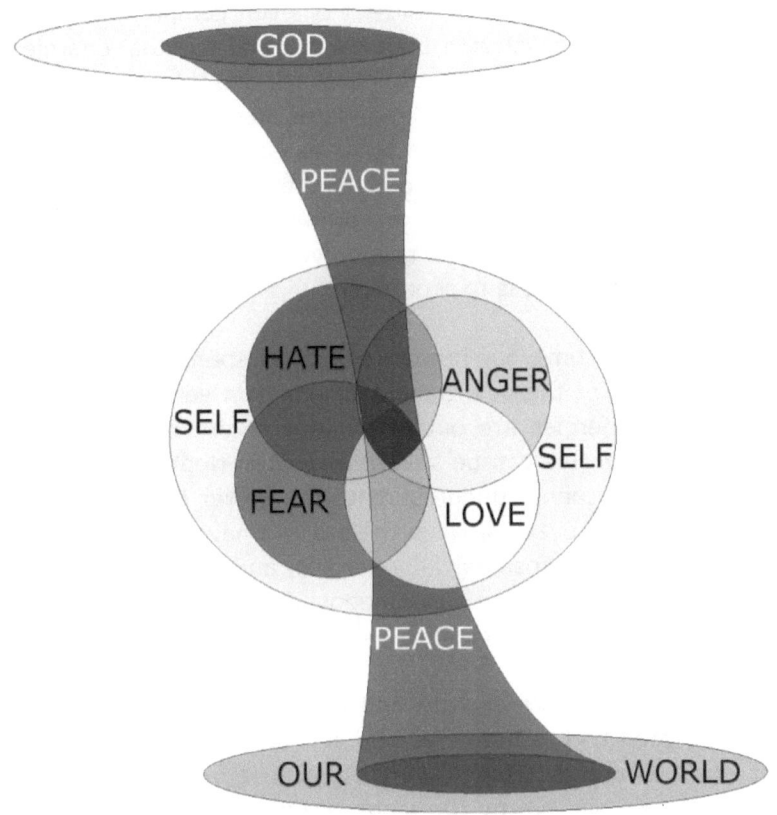

We also experience the divine energy, but this is of a very different type from our earth energy. This innate energy comes from God, through the peace that is at the center of our four core emotions. It is inborn and yet intrinsic to God. Part of what this energy brings to us is love but also curiosity, the eagerness to ask questions, to seek out answers, and to learn from them. It can also have a calming and healing effect that helps us balance ourselves against our hectic world. As mortal beings, we may never know how many ways this divine energy pulls on us or how many avenues of potential open through it.

Every day, whether we realize it or even comprehend it, we act, interact, and react with both earthly and spiritual energies. God as peace is primary to our spiritual self and is foremost in the simplest of truths. Our spiritual mandates after this are to respect each other's life and treat each other as equals. This may sound too simplified, but because of our human nature, it remains our greatest challenge. Our bodies are primary to our earthly selves. The body's prime objective is to survive and keep itself healthy, but its prime directive is to reproduce.

Most of the time our human energy is spent on needs and desires, often for the sole benefit of our own selves. Moreover, when these energies are out of balance or out of control, the repercussions for us can be severe and often ripple out to those around us. We cannot underestimate the power that our bodies and nature have over us. Nevertheless, we have been given the tools to cope with these earthly energies, and that takes us back to our spiritual selves and our relationship with God, which exists through our direct connection to the peace at our core.

As individuals, we explore and experience our world differently. As men and women, we also act, interact, and react with our world differently. This, in part, is because our bodies are different. We do not live by the same exact mix of hormones and bodily chemicals. But this does not account for everything. Males and females often-express slightly different aspects of God, but this does not make one greater than or less than the other. This subtlety of our spiritual essences is most often expressed as nurturing (female) versus guidance (male). It can also be conveyed in different non–gender-specific ways, such as inventive versus creative, conception versus perception, logic versus intuition, instinct versus reason, and even essence versus energy. Our innermost enigma is that we are all equally capable of expressing any of these natures of God.

In relation to each other, the masculine and the feminine are equally blessed in mind and spirit. They are but only, slightly different expressions of our same humanness, but they are not opposites. Neither is weaker than the other, but rather each provides strengths to offset each other's common human faults. Together they are a duet, an intertwined melody, a harmony that encompasses respect and equality, friendship and autonomy, understanding and cooperation.

Humanity's heightened level of existence is not just tied to our earthly nature but to a greater degree, our spiritual nature. As individuals, we are all capable of exhibiting a different mix of spiritual essences, and each of us is gifted with the ability to express any and all of those traits. Still, we often assign those spiritual characteristics in a certain way, often as masculine or feminine. God is neither male nor female but encompasses all those associated traits.

Within each of us, our basic spiritual nature revolves around relationships—the one we have with God and those we have with each other. This harmony is an intertwining melody of both nurturing and guidance. Within each relationship, these are some of the basic building blocks of love. By embracing the peace at our core and sharing that built-in relationship of love with others, it can move us closer to the greater whole that is God.

When we recognize how our earthly and spiritual energies intertwine to make us uniquely human, we must then accept them for what they are and admit that these natures cannot be separated while we are living. If we at least open ourselves to attempt to understand their dynamics, then we will likely learn more about ourselves. The more we know, the better we can manage our shortcomings, and we can use that knowledge to cope with our earthly demands, stresses, and hardships. Our world is too wild and too unpredictable to control. When we realize that the best we can do is manage our actions and reactions to those forces, we can then focus on the solutions that work best for us as individuals.

Truly understanding divine energy requires a different thought process. We experience this energy from the moment we are conceived and throughout our lifetime. It is derived from that conduit of peace, which passes through our core emotions. This is what connects us, not merely to our world but also to God. Enlightenment cannot start until you ask the questions and seek the answers. Awareness begins by embracing the peace at our core. However, the peace we find there is neither static nor empty. Within that conduit is a subtle movement of divine potential that is not only moving down through us from God but also up to us from our world.

This divine energy cannot be defined or possibly even tapped, but if our mind reaches a level of stillness in meditation, we can start to feel its presence passing through. Here we can let go of our inner turmoil and release our intentions and desires into the stream that is that conduit of peace that passes through our core. Within the stillness, we can listen. If we are patient and our soul is at ease, the wisdom and the richness of both God and the earth will gather around us.

Eye of the Hurricane

Whether you know it or even accept it, God is the core of your being, and it is a deeply peaceful, eternally quiet, and timelessly still place. God is the eye of the hurricane that is your life, and you are the wild energy spinning around it. Without this peaceful core, we stop turning, we stop moving, and we cease to exist as enlightened people.

Below the hurricane, which is you, is water, and this is the world we live in. You have been drawn out of this ocean and have been made self-aware. No longer are you wholly immersed in this sea of life, and yet you can never entirely be separated from it. Forever estranged from this ocean, you are still water, but in a different form. As a living being, you cannot exist without water. The sea sustains you; you draw your energy from it and release your energy back into it. To an extent, it has some control over you, but through the gifts of self-awareness and reasoning, it is never total control.

Above you are the steering winds. They are the jet streams of unconscious thoughts and free will. Every thought and every choice you make affects the direction you move throughout the ever-changing course of your life. God lifts you up and is the stillness at your center. The world is at your feet and sustains you, but it is your free will that sets you in motion. You create your own path, and ultimately, your journey begins and ends with you.

Most of the time, we are just small, harmless bundles of energy bumping into each another. What most people fail to realize is that when you choose to hold on to anger, hate, sorrow, or fear—whether it is a conscious or an unconscious choice—you slowly move over turbulent waters. That turbulence affects the decisions you make and influences your choices thereafter. The consequences can send you spinning, fueling a storm within you.

Whereas emotions are internal reactions and ultimately choices you make, desire is the direct result of the influence the water (our world) has on you. Desire in and of itself is not a bad thing. As you react to its pull, the real danger comes when you allow it to consume your thoughts and overpower your will. If allowed, this uncontrolled desire will draw you off course; it will pull you down into what is most likely an intensely stormy sea. Our uncontrolled desire for power, money, sex, or any other earthly thing started with a choice and in turn skewed every decision thereafter. In the end, it affects not only you but also those closest to you and potentially others.

Between our internal and external struggles, we all have the capacity to spin up and become a Category 5 hurricane, which can cause massive damage to ourselves, those around us, and any others we may slam into along the way. Once the damage is done, it is not easily repaired or cannot be mended at all, and the forgiveness, healing, and rebuilding can often take a long time.

With every choice you make, there are side effects, for good or bad, and these effects have consequences for you and those around you. Those consequences can alter the paths we each follow and can leave you and others with few choices or none at all. We may be forced to accept a new course and its destination, whether you intended it or not, whether you understand it or not.

Every bump and every ripple we create through our own decisions, actions, and words can affect others. Through these actions, we can just as quickly send one or many bundles of energy spinning out of control or nudge another back onto a safer course. Sometimes we are aware of these slight bumps and nudges, but generally, most happen beyond the scope of our vision, without any knowledge they ever occurred. Bumps, nudges, and collisions happen because we are all sharing the same space and moving over the same ocean. What is most important is what we do after we collide.

So what do we do at this point? It is God's hope that we look into ourselves, find the peace that is at our center, and embrace it. For us to release our anger, our hate, and our fear into the quietness and let the stillness calm them. To allow this deep peace to help us let go of our hurt and our pain by letting that heaviness lift from our hearts and fly away into the emptiness. For us to ask for forgiveness and to forgive so, we can unburden our souls, allowing us to trust ourselves and trust the choices we must make every day. To find the strength to seek the timeless serenity and ask for help balancing our desires with our needs and to fix our gaze toward this peace and give thanks. For us to have the courage in those hard times, to let go of our free will and trust God even when we are not sure of our course or where a new path will take us. To say to ourselves and believe that all things lay within us, and peace is our epicenter.

Walking Out of the Dark: Part One

Deep Is My Ocean

Depression has set over the dark sea of my mind, I am adrift.

Swept by raging winds, tossed upon the churning waters, sinking into the emptiness, I am alone.

The living day has ended, the dreaming night has gone, darkness beneath the surface, I am lost.

Suspended in nowhere, no bottom no top, just numbing cold water and lungs burning for air, I am nothing.

Caught by a receding tide, pounded by retreating waves, weakly struggling in the liquid sand, I am hurting.

Under a foggy moonless night, on a barren strip of land, clinging to the jagged rocks, I am broken.

In the East the sunrise, the horizon blood red, darkness in battle retreats, I am crying.

The surf crashes at my feet, its sound roars in my ears, I am motionless.

The light warms my skin, a fresh breeze fills my lungs, I am healing.

Standing on a high cliff, blue sky above, looking over the calm water, I am reborn.

But, fast are the days, long are the nights and deep is my ocean.

Arthur woke chilled, not in the sense of being cold; he was perfectly warm under his blanket. Yet, unlike most mornings when he became aware of his surroundings, and the realities of his situation took hold of him again, he would resolve to face the day, to do something positive to change his circumstances. This morning brought feelings long buried, deep from his past. Flashes of happier times flooded over him. Then the overwhelming sense of loss and helplessness from the days after his mum passed way washed over him.

Whenever those feeling surfaced, as they did this morning, it sometimes led him to think about his father. Yet, as hard as he tried, those memories had faded. What remained was a sensation, one that he could not associate with anything specific. He quickly cleared his mind and pushed out those grief-stricken thoughts. For whenever those strong predawn cloudbursts of emotions washed over him, they always seemed to precede something terrible. A deep foreboding settled into his stomach. What was it going to be this time—how many setbacks, how many more disappointments must he have to face?

The smell of something good from downstairs made his stomach rumble. His aunt was up and, as always, working tirelessly in the kitchen, baking most likely. Arthur thought of his aunt and uncle. They had always been kind to him. He really did feel that they loved him as their own. They always made him feel safe, and for that, he was grateful and would do almost anything for them.

Hunger finally won, so Arthur quickly washed up and dressed and then headed downstairs to the kitchen. Upon entering, he found Aunt Kaisa standing on a chair, straining to reach something on the top shelf of the pantry. "Let me help you with that," Arthur said. Then, without thinking, he sprinted across the kitchen. Just as he arrived, his aunt lost her balance. He instinctively reached and steadied her.

"My gracious, you have always had a way about you," she said.

"I'm sorry, I should not have run up and startled you..." Arthur was cut off before he could finish.

"Oh dear me, I didn't mean it that way. If you had not acted as quickly as you did, you would have watched this stubborn old woman fall off this chair. What I meant is that you, Arthur, have always had a way about you. Here you are, up earlier than I've seen you up in God knows how long, as if you sensed I was going to need help this morning. I've had the pleasure of watching you grow up and have seen you do similar kinds of things on several occasions with the most unlikely of people."

Arthur said nothing, but he must have had an odd look on his face. His aunt stepped down from the chair and reached up, patted him on the cheek, and said, "Ponder on that for a while, my dear boy. Think about it," she added. "Now I need to go get your lazy uncle out of bed."

Arthur set the small corner table in the kitchen, grabbed the butter and preserves from the icebox, began to slice the warm bread, and sat down to wait. After a short time had gone by, and his aunt still had not returned with his uncle, he crammed a big bite of bread into his mouth and went to find out what was taking them so long.

The moment he stepped into their bedroom, the soul-crushing scene was forever burned into his memory as his mind struggled to take it all in. There, lying across her husband's chest was his aunt, quietly weeping. At that moment, the bread in Arthur's mouth may as well have been sawdust, and he tried hard to swallow it through a rising sob. Even though he felt the dark memories of his past surrounding him, he reached out to his aunt. She flung her arm around his waist and clung to him. Through her sobs, she moaned that Zachary had only said he was tired and needed to rest a little longer. He must have passed away while she was baking.

* * *

A few days later, Arthur's uncle was buried in the cemetery not far from the inn that his aunt and uncle owned, the only home Arthur had ever known. On the walk back to the inn, Arthur's aunt held tightly to his arm. A short distance ahead of them was the inn's maid, Olena, and her daughter, Mairwyn. Arthur's aunt and uncle had taken them in after Olena's husband had left them, and they had lost their home. They had lived in one of the rooms on the top floor of the inn since Mairwyn was a toddler.

"You know," his aunt said after a long stretch of silence. "Your uncle and I don't really own the inn." Arthur stopped in his tracks. "The inn was your father's, and when your mother died, it was left to you." She let out a long sigh. "There is not a day that goes by that I don't miss my little sis." She turned, smiled, and patted Arthur on the cheek. "But I have you, and that makes every day much brighter."

A thousand thoughts raced through Arthur's mind in the seconds that followed. Arthur's aunt tugged on his arm, and they started walking again. "Don't look so horrified. It's not like I'm asking you to take over the inn," she said and paused before continuing, "and the brickworks today. Besides, your mother—God bless her soul—she knew enough to make some other arrangements for you."

"What do you mean? And I would never take the inn from you. It's...it's your home!"

She kept her eye on the crowd ahead of them. "Mairwyn has grown into a fine young lady, don't you think?" She had very purposely changed the subject, and Arthur knew it.

"I guess so, but—"

"I think she may be the one who will miss you the most," she said and paused again. "When you are away at the university."

"What?" Arthur tried to stop again, but his aunt had kept a tight grip on his arm and kept him moving forward.

"Before your mum passed, she purchased two certificates that would guarantee two years at the university down in the capital. Over the years, your uncle and I were able to buy two more certificates for you. Four years should get you a degree of some sort. Use the gift wisely, my dear Arthur. Use it wisely."

As they turned the corner and started across the courtyard to the inn, his aunt stopped. "This inn and the brickworks are yours, Arthur; I will look after them until you return. Then you can decide what you want to do with them." Before Arthur could protest, she went on. "Now, let's go inside and join our friends gathered in memory of your uncle, and a have a bit of lunch," she said. "Are you ready?" she asked and nodded toward the door.

Inside the inn, the gathering was quite large. Many people from the village and surrounding area had shown up to pay their respects to Arthur's uncle, Zachary. Many offered to help Kaisa and Arthur in any way they could.

For Arthur, the next few hours passed quickly. Though, through most of that time, two things kept playing at the corner of his mind. The first was Mairwyn. Granted, they had grown up together, and they always seemed to get along okay, but generally, they hung out in their own circles of friends. Yet today, she was never more than a few steps away and seemed determined to help him or get anything he needed. In fact, ever since his uncle had passed away, she seemed to have attached herself to him. Arthur hadn't really given it much of a thought until the conversation with his aunt that morning. The other, more pressing matter was the idea of attending the university. Although the thought of it was exciting, Arthur didn't like the prospect of moving down to the capital. He loved his village and the inn. They were his home. The city seemed cold and intimidating, and the idea of spending four years there was genuinely frightening.

* * *

Over the following weeks, the anticipation of heading off to the university dominated Arthur's every waking thought. But he was determined to make his mum, aunt, and uncle proud and pressed forward as if it were to be his greatest adventure.

Section 2

Freeway of Life

Equality does not mean every car on the freeway of life moving at the same speed with the same distance between each vehicle. If that were the case, no one would be able to merge onto the freeway or change lanes to exit. Equality is respecting the other drivers on the road and understanding that they all have a different destination in mind as well as their own course and pace to get them there. The goal is not how fast we move or the distance we are traveling; instead, it is about getting where we want to go safely. It is about having the integrity to not only watch out for all those other drivers throughout our own journey but also to give them the opportunity to move and maneuver on the freeway. It is about having the wisdom to know when to speed up, when to change lanes when to pass, when to slow down, and when to stop.

The Simplest of Truths

So what is it that drives us, what has made humankind successful? Looking back into the vagueness of our past, some might suggest, at first glance, that success lies within a culture, a way of life. Others might argue that our persistent desire or need to believe in a higher power played a crucial role in our success. Both of these ideas may be partially right, but we need to look further back, to what got us to those points in the first place.

We are creatures of habit, good and bad. Our daily habits become routines, and our routines become a way of life. As we pass these lifestyles on to our children over generations, they become our family traditions. Now, connect this to humankind's fiercely tribal nature, and those traditions become our culture. Often, our religious philosophy is steeped in our traditions and our culture, and those infused beliefs become part of our greater identity. In truth, our faith is often defined by our culture. It shapes—and continues to influence—why and how we believe in a higher power. So looking even further back, what is it then that has really defined our success?

The first and most important gift we have received from God is awareness, both self and situational. From out of this awareness evolved our ability to reason, to think beyond the moment and plan for tomorrow. It enabled us to look for better ways of doing things and then gave us the means to pass along this new knowledge. This is what defines and separates us from other animals. Yet the real drive behind our success, when you look back on early humanity, is our adaptability—our willingness to change our existing behaviors and adapt them to new situations. This is what has enabled us to survive even in the harshest environments.

We have been made self-aware and have been enlightened. We have never stopped adapting and changing, even as we continue reaching for new levels of understanding. This ability comes directly from the divine potential that lies at the core of our being. What you find when you look at humanity today is that our habits and routines, and even our culture and religion, can become barriers when faced with a slowly and continuously changing world and our increasingly global society. We often do not recognize, or we just choose to ignore that change is the one constant in our world. Change and adaptation are what drives our ever-inquisitive mind.

Whether we accept this or not, change is a constant, and everything changes slowly over time: the universe, our planet, our environment, and even our cultures and religions. When looking at the last two, most of our traditions, customs, rituals, ceremonies, sacraments, and sacred objects started as a way to help us remember an event or pass on bits of knowledge and wisdom. In the worst cases, they are nothing more than propaganda that has circulated through history with no real grounding in truth.

As we look at different factors of change—for example, when similar cultures and religions become isolated from each other—shifts will naturally start to occur. Language is an excellent example of markers of change. Compounded by the obscurity of a long period of time, customs or traditions can change slightly to fit a newer interpretation. This may occur because of a limited understanding of the rationale of their origins. Other, more forceful factors of change can come in the form of conquest or natural disasters.

As the generations go by, the more likely bits and pieces are added, changed, or removed from our traditions and ceremonies. Variances not only happen because of distance and time but by accident or on purpose. Someone of authority may not like certain aspects of a tradition and force a change. Original manuscripts may have been hidden for safekeeping only to become lost. Others may have been miscopied, degraded beyond usefulness, or were destroyed.

Inconsistencies can also happen when the guardians of wisdom die young, resulting in vital information being lost. Knowledge may not be passed on correctly to the next generation because it was misunderstood or misinterpreted. The effect can be a tradition or ceremony that is broader in scope and no longer resembles or even functions as originally intended. It may have also passed beyond any real relevance.

At some point, it became our cultures, and to a greater extent our religions, that most closely bound together significant populations of humanity. Yet so often, these ethnic or religious groups fall back on intolerance to elevate and advance themselves. From within the many layers of our cultures and religions stem traditions, customs, rituals, ceremonies, sacraments, and even sacred objects that can promote a narrow-minded viewpoint. It is this prejudice that distracts us from the authentic path to God. When we are unwilling or too arrogant to ask the questions that allow us to evaluate how what, and why we believe or weigh the effects of our beliefs, it directly results in our failure to understand the actual consequences, not just on ourselves but more importantly on others, or even the effect on our direct relationship with God.

When we are no longer willing to accept change in any form, then we have stripped ourselves of the ability to see the dangers of our ways. Our inflexibility and intolerance are the root cause of so much suffering in the world. This is what places the highest debt on our souls. To put it simply, we have injected so much of our humanity and our culture into our religions and made these ideologies so sacred that we can no longer accept the simplest of truths without putting our own qualifiers on them.

Our ability to reason and adapt has made us very successful, but it is in our success that the roots of our most serious faults can be found. Success can make us complacent, arrogant, and ignorant. Complacency in our habits and routines can make us inflexible or resistant to change. Our arrogance leads us to believe that our way of life is better than our neighbors', and therefore, we are better.

In ignorance, we elevate traditions that discriminate against or even harm others and then blindly or passionately defend them as sacred. Invariably, when there is disparity and intolerance problems arise, whether it is between men and women, different individuals, cultures or religions, and yet we still habitually fall back on the one lesson we know best. The world we live in is unrelenting and unforgiving, and as a result, we have learned to kill or be killed. It then becomes not the survival of the fittest or wisest but rather, survival of the most hostile and brutal.

We will stop at nothing to protect ourselves, our families, and to an equal extent, our traditions and way of life, regardless of where the threat or perceived threat originated. We can be as uncaring, unforgiving, and unrelenting as nature. These are our biggest hurdles and likely the roots of our own extinction. This is what obscures and obstructs our path to peace and God. Yet in all this, we have been given the tools to overcome these shortcomings.

We all need to take a hard look at our religious and cultural traditions and honestly weigh them against the simplest of truths. When we do this can we start to recognize any injustice that hides within them. Once we start this process, we need to follow through and take steps to make collaborative efforts to change them. This is what will make us better people. We cannot and should not hold on to any traditions for the sake of culture if it promotes inequality and injustice or violates the rights of others or the sanctity of life.

We are all capable of listening with our hearts for the guidance that can help us find the right path, but the fact is, we often do not. That is because tradition and culture can push us down its own path. So how many times must God send messengers out among us, to repeat the same message over and over again? How many chances will we be given to turn away from our arrogant and self-serving ideologies and cultures of entitlement that discriminate against or persecute our neighbors? Ultimately, it is our own stubborn inflexibility that turns us away from peace and from God, even more so when that intolerance stems from our religious dogma or psyche.

How many times will God intercede on our behalf? The answer is as many times as it will take to prevent us from annihilating each other. God will never purposely destroy humanity. However, because of the volatile nature of our humanity and our world, catastrophic events happen. That risk has always existed, and the potential for more will continue. Still, God remains truly vested in us, always ready to guide us forward.

God is not complicated. We make God complicated. Each one of us has the ability to ask the questions that will allow us to seek the higher path, and we each have a responsibility to ask those questions. God has given us another gift that is directly connected to and is equally important as the first but, for the most part, goes unnoticed. Hidden at the core of every person is a quiet place, an ocean of profound stillness, the presence of which can be overwhelming. This peacefulness is God. This feeling of peace or peacefulness is the closest we will ever get to tangible proof for the existence of God.

True peace is sensed from within. It bypasses our senses, which mainly connects us to our environment and our world. Religions often limit us to live God from the outside in, which in turn can allow the corruptive factors of culture and tradition to overshadow the simplest of truths. Embracing the peace at our core puts God at our center, allowing each of us to live God from the inside out. By living this way, we each have a greater potential to influence our own families, our own communities, and, from there, all of humanity.

These simplest of truths are the essence of God embedding in us and our humanity, it is the code we should teach our children and follow every day of our lives.

1. **God is the core of your being. Remember to draw your strength from the peace within.**

2. **Your life and the lives of your neighbors are sacred. Protect and help one another.**

3. **God does not distinguish man from woman nor one color of skin from another. We are all equal. Respect one another.**

The Simplest of Truths

Any religion across the globe that cannot embrace and live by these simplest of truths is indeed nothing more than an ideology based on cultural conditions and has no real value or relevance to God.

Mass Transit

In our fast-paced modern lifestyle, nothing represents our independence and freedom more than the vehicles we drive. However, when it comes to our beliefs and our religions, we are more likely to be one of many travelers crowded into a mass-transit system. Now, there is nothing wrong with taking the bus or riding the train, but we have to do this with the confidence that we will get to our destination safely. We want to know before we step into that bus, train, or airplane that it has been well-built, it is well-maintained, and it is reliable.

If we are going to put our lives, our faith, onto a mass-transit system, we do so with the expectation that the system is managed wisely and that its engineers are honest and responsible. That they are well-trained and dedicated to their job and have a professional and caring attitude, not only toward those traveling with them but also toward those, who are not. The most significant difference here is that we typically do not voluntarily step into a religion. We are born on that bus or train through our parents. We spend our whole lives on that vehicle learning the rules of being a good passenger. The inherent risk is that we can become too comfortable, closing our eyes to the world outside our windows, an unconscious passenger blindly going along for the ride.

If we are not careful, we can be led to believe or lulled into thinking that ours is the only vehicle that can get us to God. With this type of logic, there is a genuine risk that the scope of our vision and our mind can become too narrowly focused. When this happens, we no longer see or care about the harm we are doing to the people who are not riding with us.

When the windows of our bus or train are painted over, and we are taught not to question what we are told, we are at risk of being led astray. When we are instructed to believe without question, in the context of absolutes, we need to pause, take a closer look, and ask ourselves these questions about each belief: Does it interfere with my relationship with God, or is it even relevant? Does it discriminate against or disrespect me or any other people on or off my bus? Does this violate the sanctity of life?

We all have a responsibility to keep the windows on our bus or plane clean and to ensure that our vehicle is well maintained, moving at a safe speed, and headed in the right direction. Without a clear and unobstructed view, it is not uncommon for our religious will to be bent away from, or be in stark contrast to, the will of God. This is because our religious views are often based on a cultural bias that limits the amount and type of information we are given.

We need to continually analyze the information we are given and be aware of its source, from who is saying it, and how it is being presented. To do this, we need to educate ourselves on how to scrutinize information by comparing it to the simplest of truths. When we do, we can then recognize when the information is off base or too narrow in its scope to be entirely valid. Each of us has a responsibility to ask the difficult questions and then empower ourselves to make course corrections. Especially when we find that information goes blatantly against the simplest of truths.

We all have the right to the truth, and we have the right to seek the whole truth, but we all have a greater responsibility, to be honest in that endeavor. We must push each other to be alert and conscientious passengers, vigilant in our faith and the course of that faith. The more mindful we are of how it relates to others, the better we will be in evaluating our actions—those of our faith and of our leaders. When we do this, we can then recognize the errors of our ways and make honest attempts to correct them.

So why is it that we are so willing to ignore the obvious omission, the extreme prejudice, or the blatant cruelty that come when someone or something is contrary to our beliefs? Why is it that we can act so violently against someone who is strong enough to stand up and question the direction and speed the bus or plane is traveling? The answer is just that no one wants to admit or hear that his or her sacred, long-held beliefs might be flawed. It is easier to label someone, or some society, or even a different religious philosophy as blasphemous or evil than to honestly measure their merits.

Change does not always mean changing our cultural values, but rather, reaching an understanding that allows a dialogue. It is harder still to set aside our biases so we can find common ground. Yet if we can do this, we will likely see that rooted in both are the simplest of truths, and this is something that all sides should be able to embrace as the common ground. After that, the rest is just social differences, and if we can accept these, then a door will be opened for more peaceful coexistence.

Our beliefs are not always going to be the same as our neighbors because we are widely diverse people, and our customs and values are different. However, when we or our neighbors try and force our own beliefs on others, and it violates their or our fundamental human rights or causes harm, then we have dishonored the two mandates of the simplest of truths. In doing this, we have defied God. Intolerance is not the way to defend and uphold a truth, or a principle, or moralities because by acting in this way we generate our own spiritual debt. Tolerance does not mean sacrificing your beliefs, rather, it should be looked at as a way to avoid added burdens on our own soul.

Tolerance does not start with understanding and then acceptance. Instead, tolerance begins by putting aside your biases and acknowledging the differences. You may never agree or understand someone's stance on a subject, but you can let them live their life on their own terms. So long as each of us lives our lives through the simplest of truths, that being peace, equality and to uphold and value the sanctity of life. Through this we can find a level of harmony in our society. However, we cannot and should never separate, segregate or isolate people who are different from us. This builds barriers which shut down communication and ultimately undermine any chance we have of understanding each other.

In the end, we will all be judged by our actions and held accountable for them. Whether our intentions were right or not, if we have acted against our neighbor and caused him or her pain, then we have created a debt. Every debt that we create and do not seek forgiveness for in our lifetime will be paid in full during our final judgment. Because it is as essential to forgive as it is to be forgiven, every debt we fail to forgive in our lifetime will also be held against us in our final judgment.

The first part of the simplest of truths tells us to put God and peace first. The last two are mandates on how we should interact with each other. When we all accept and embrace God and peace as our core and strive to treat each other as sacred and equal, then the number of vehicles to drive us toward our goal can be as varied as the many mass-transit systems in our world today.

Since each of us has a personal connection to God and peace, then the number of paths will be as many as the number of people in our world. This is how it has to be because God knows that no one religion can become the sole mass-transit system to peace without becoming entirely corrupted by the worldly powers of prestige, privilege, and affluence that is gained through the complete control they can exert over their faithful. Our spiritual diversity then becomes our first level of defense against the forces of corruption. Unfortunately, through our own shortsightedness, we continue to allow our cultural arrogance, religious self-righteousness, and intolerance to power the gears of hate and conflict.

Traffic

Even before we earned our driver's license, we had to learn how to deal with the traffic in our lives. It is interesting, when you stop and think about it, how that one card becomes a powerful expression of independence and freedom. Undeniably, nothing related to driving is free, but if you have the resources, you can go as far as the road can take you. For some, they push it even further, to where there are no roads.

However, the reality is that we will always have to contend with some level of traffic in our lives. For many, it is a daily ride through frustration. For others, it is only an occasional journey into chaos. When you think about it, just as the driver's license can be an expression of independence and freedom, driving and dealing with traffic can be a metaphor for life and living.

When it comes to driving, there may be nothing more annoying than having to sit at a traffic light, stop sign, or just in heavy traffic, because, to our mind, cars were not designed to sit idle. Cars were made to get us from point A to point B, as fast as possible.

Admit it—we have all watched other drivers and likely done it ourselves. We speed from stoplight to stoplight, with hardly a thought of a turn signal, as we zip around car after car. In the process, we may only get one or two car lengths ahead before the next stoplight. So why is it that we seem to have a restless need to get around every vehicle in front of us? Maybe we are in a hurry and do not like being forced to drive at another driver's pace. Perhaps we are just seeking an unobstructed view of the road ahead. Maybe we want the freedom of the empty road. The reality is that at almost every point along our journey, there will be some sort of traffic. If we ever do happen to come close to that goal of racing down that wide-open highway, we might just discover that we are now alone.

No matter how many cars we pass or stoplights we run through, eventually, we will need to use the brakes. For every green light we roll through in life, a red one will cause us to slow down and stop. On some days there will be more green lights and on other days more red ones. What we need to remember is that there will always be some fluctuation in our pace. The problem is that we become so easily distracted by these minor starts and stops that we lose track of our goal; that is, to make it to our destination safely and allow others to do the same.

However, it is in our nature not to remember all the green lights we made it through, but rather to get angry with the ones where we did not. With all likelihood, the harder we try to ram our way through the traffic the more frustrated, and angry we become, and the more we anger the drivers around us. The result can be that those other drivers are less likely to give you room to maneuver, and fewer opportunities will open up in traffic.

We never stop and think about how our actions on the road of life may have affected the other drivers. How we may have been the root cause of another driver's bad day, or worse, caused someone else's accident. We are only concerned with the few minutes we shaved off our drive time. That is, at least, until someone else cuts us off, and we spill coffee in our lap.

Living in our modern world has made many people impatient and selfish. It is a world of instant gratification. We feel empowered when we are behind the wheel. We have places to go and a road to conquer—let no one stand in our way. In our daily quest to get there and back again, we drive at our own pace, often without a thought of the speed we are traveling, the rules of the road, or much concern for the drivers around us.

The more routine our path, the more we tie ourselves to a particular course, and the less likely we are to deviate from it. That everyday drive becomes second nature, and it lulls us into becoming too comfortable behind the wheel. Taking into consideration the distractions we also have inside our vehicles, we can quickly reach a point where we find ourselves in trouble when road conditions change.

We often forget that change is the one constant on the road and in our lives. Unexpected detours may prevent you from taking your daily route, or the traffic will not allow you the opportunity to change lanes so you can catch the off-ramp or make your next turn. Our inattention or impatience pushes us through the yellow or red light. Our stubbornness in that routine compels us to make that unprotected left turn, across three lanes of heavy traffic, even though we know it would be safer to drive to the next stoplight and approach that destination from a different direction. The combination of these occurrences and our shortsighted behaviors can throw us off balance ever so slightly and lead to an unfortunate turn of events on the road of life.

The point is not to let yourself become so comfortable behind the wheel that driving becomes a distraction to everything else you are trying to do. We should never forget that other drivers surround us and that we need to look out for them as much as we need to look out for ourselves. We need to prevent ourselves from being so ingrained in a route or the course we have planned that we lose sight of the fact that there is always more than one way to reach our destination. We all need to stay focused on the road and on the vehicles around us and be flexible in our route. Being in the driver's seat should be about staying focused but flexible.

The drive is about the path you travel, the route that gets you to your destination regardless of the traffic or detours. Driving is about the attitude you take to get there. It is realizing that it is not just about you, but how you act and react to everything going on around you at every point along your journey. Living, like driving, is about being prepared for change, adapting to it, and moving on—even if it means taking a route you did not plan on. At these times, we need to reassure ourselves that with the right amount of *drive*, we *will* arrive at our destination. Driving, like living, is learning to harmonize with the people around you. It is realizing that they also have a path they are traveling and accepting that everyone's course, pace, and perspective is different. So what kind of driver are you?

Walking out of the Dark: Part Two

Fires of Hate

*Anger strikes like a lightning bolt,
splitting the air with a hiss and a deafening blast.*

*Resentment smolders in the charred wound
of the thunderbolt's fierce blow.*

*Enmity and bitterness, it seethes and fumes in the
growing strength of the heat's hostility.*

*Hate blossoms into flame as it feeds on the petulance
of a drought-plagued land.*

*Wrath, vehemence, and violence whirl in the wildfire
as its frenzied forcefulness increases.*

*Fury rages in the firestorm where nothing is spared
from the ferocity of the inferno.*

*Fear and panic hang like the choking smoke
that lingers above the scorched earth.*

*Sorrow and sadness fall like a crying rain on the desolation
of the once beautiful land.*

*Mourning Time it alone remembers what once was
but also sees what eventually will be.*

*Hope springs up with the newness of life,
for the fire of hate can never destroy*

The Simplest of Truths

*Nature's loving Spirit or the fertileness
of Life's rich Potential.*

Arthur woke with the image of his mum's face fading from his mind. He was more than cold—stiff, painfully sore in many places, and numb in others. His head throbbed, and for a while, he could not put his thoughts in order. Opening his eyes did not help; it was dark, and he could not think of where he could possibly be. With a bit of effort, he made himself relax and replay everything from the start of the day. What was the first thing he could remember about this morning?

Everyone at the university seemed to have the same thing on his or her mind this morning. A massive march had been planned to protest the rampant corruption in the government and the king, who seemed to be ignoring the people's hardship and suffering. Then, all in a rush, everything came flooding back to memory...the peaceful march breaking down in chaos after the police's and later the army's arrival.

The scene played out in Arthur's head in a blur. There were images of protesters being shot and killed. People were running in all directions, and others being trampled. As if in slow motion, he saw the face of a little girl running toward him and then saw her chest explode as a bullet tore through her. A moment later, she was face down in the street. Tears ran down into Arthur's ears as an old, familiar, gnawing feeling swept over him and settled in his stomach. He had gotten himself into a very dreadful situation. Arthur tried to sit up.

"The dead rises," said a raspy voice. "Don't move. I will come to you." There was a shuffling of feet, and a dirty and very foul-smelling man emerged from the darkness. "Easy now, don't try to get up yet. You've got quite a goose egg on your head."

The old man crouched down next to Arthur. "Listen to me. I've heard far too much here in this place tonight. More than my sober mind can handle." He pointed to the door. "I can't help those poor souls out there, but maybe I can help you."

"I know I am a worthless drunk," he said as he started digging through a worn and dirty sack. "But that doesn't make me any less feeling or less of a person." He turned back to Arthur. "I have a bit of a plan, you see. I've got some extra clothes—they might be a bit big, but that'll be okay. Here, let me help you sit up. You'll need to get into these clothes as quickly as you can before, you know, they come back." The old man jerked his head toward the door.

Before who gets back? Thought Arthur as the knot grew in his belly. Something stirred inside him, and it set his hands in motion.

"No, no clean white skivvies," said the bum, "could give you away."

The clothes Arthur put on reeked, and between the smell and his churning stomach, he threw up on himself. The old man laughed. "Nice touch," he said. "I think you might be safe, for now. Let's hope they just think you're another old drunk like me. Here, let me help you lay down again and try to get some rest."

Arthur lay there watching the old man push his clothes to the bottom of his bag and shuffle back into the darkness. The bum may have been out of sight, but he talked endlessly. He told Arthur that they were in the holding cell for the drunks and homeless vagrants. He described how Arthur had been dragged in and unceremoniously dumped in the middle of the cell, and that the guards had talked about coming back for him later.

The old beggar talked about all the things he had heard throughout the night, the horrible sounds that were broken only by gunshots. Arthur lost track of how many times the old man said he needed a stiff drink.

"You know at first, when they brought you in here, I thought you were dead," said the bum. "When you started showing signs of life, I decided I had to do something. I pulled you over to one of the darker corners so they wouldn't see you right away. Then a plan started to grow in my head. But I couldn't figure out how

I was going to get my old clothes on you. Then, just when I was thinking about giving up, you woke up. Problem solved."

The bum continued talking, and Arthur tried tuning him out. More than anything he just wanted to go back to sleep, but his mind was swimming in a sea of thoughts. Those familiar and random memories of his mum were back; even the shadowy ones of his father were there. Then the sounds that the old man had described earlier, the screaming and the gunshots, started again. Those of women sobbing and wailing seemed to cut into his very soul.

All of the sad feelings from the darkest moments of his childhood were back, to herald the awful things yet to come. As if that were not enough, the absolute fear and dread he felt in his current situation threatened to make his heart explode out of his chest. The old man was murmuring loudly to himself over in his corner. *The sun must be coming up*, thought Arthur, for there was just enough light coming in through the small window to let Arthur see that the old man had both hands over his ears trying to block out the screaming, but with every gunshot, he would jump and cringe.

Arthur tried thinking of other things. His mind drifted back to that first year at the university and how hard that transition had been on him. Most of the students were from wealthy families, and they almost entirely ignored him. It was a strange feeling; he had never had a problem making friends back in his village, and although he had many acquaintances at the university, he had no real friendships.

He knew that he would have probably never finished his first year if it had not been for the letters he received from his aunt and, to his surprise, Mairwyn. At first, he felt that his aunt was making the girl write those letters, but over several months, he realized that Mairwyn's letters were very genuine. She wrote more often than his aunt did, and her letters always seemed to show up when he needed some cheering up. Writing her was easy, and by the end of his first year, he felt he could write to her about almost anything.

The sound of the jail door sliding open with a bang startled Arthur out of his thoughts so severely that he felt his bladder betray him. It was now full daylight beyond the small window that gave some light to the cell. A man strode in, and his uniform was splattered with blood. He stopped in the center of the room and then turned toward the bum. He said nothing but slowly pulled out a pistol and took aim at him. Arthur tried to yell, but only a cough came out. The man spun around and pointed the gun at Arthur's head. He froze in fear. It was the field marshal. To Arthur, it could be no other, with his firm-set jaw, the arrogant expression, and the lifeless, stone-cold eyes. He was the one who'd given the order to fire on the protesters and the one who had shot the little girl.

At that point, the chief constable walked into the cell. The field marshal turned to meet the constable and then put the gun squarely between his eyes. "Where is the piece of scum I had dragged in here?"

The bum spoke first. "Your men came and got him a while back."

"*Whose* men?" yelled the field marshal, "the constable's men, or mine?"

"I don't know," said the bum. "I'm drunk, and it was dark."

The field marshal turned and pointed the gun again at the bum. "Who is this...this *thing*, Constable?"

"A vagrant. He goes by Philthy. He is a bit of a regular."

"And that one?" With a sweep of his arm, the gun was back on Arthur.

"I was here when they brought Philthy in," said Arthur with a cough, not recognizing his own hoarse and raspy voice. The chief constable turned and glared at Arthur but said nothing.

There was a long silence. Then the field marshal slipped the pistol back into its holster. "Bring these two dregs along," he said to the constable as he walked out of the cell. "It's time to take out the garbage."

The rest of the day, Philthy and Arthur were put to work hauling out the dead from the precinct jail. They piled the bodies in a covered troop transport trailer and then rode on the macabre heap of twisted and tortured souls far out into the countryside.

By the time they had unloaded the truck, Arthur's mind was numb. He couldn't honestly say that he knew any of the people he had dumped into the mass grave, though he thought he recognized some as being students. But whether he remembered them or not, none had done anything to deserve to die so horribly. They were in the ditch when the chief constable stepped up to the edge.

"I was supposed to shoot both of you once the work was done, but I do not want to see any more death today. I am going to fire two rounds in the side of the ditch; wait a few minutes while I distract the remaining officers and soldiers and then make a run for the woods. Good luck, and Phil, don't even think about coming back to the city."

The chief constable then pulled out his revolver and fired two rounds. The shots were so close to their heads that both of them jumped for cover at the bottom of the ditch. After the sound of voices had faded into the distance, they peeked over the edge. No one seemed to be around. Once Arthur and Philthy were out of the ditch, they ran.

After they were far enough away from the mass grave and could run no longer, they stopped for a short rest. Arthur asked if Philthy knew of his village. Philthy nodded.

"Can you convey a message to my aunt who runs the inn there?" Philthy nodded again. "When you get there, just ask for Kaisa. I also need you to stay sober...at least until you can deliver my message."

Arthur paused and looked around, wondering what to do next. He turned back to Philthy. "I know it is a lot to ask, but can you do this for me?" Philthy seem to go pale in the cheeks, but he replied that he would do it.

By now, Arthur's mind was on fire; it burned with hate he had never felt before, and he vowed to do whatever he could to make the field marshal, the one with the stone-cold eyes, pay for his crimes.

Section 3

Inside Out

God does not always simply grant prayers or provide miracles in your life or in adversity. Instead, God provides opportunities. You can endlessly pray and ask why life is harsh and cruel. Or you can uncover the peace that lies within and allow it to strengthen you. You can limit yourself to live behind fear and helplessness and just wait for something good to happen. Or you can bravely reach out, embrace the opportunities in front of you, and make the most of them. You can plead and cry or be bitter and angry at the bad things or unanswered prayers and then rebuff God. Or you can listen through meditation and allow that inner-compass, your peaceful core to be the central force for change. You can live your life solely and uncompromisingly by your own needs, wants, and desires. Or live your life with compassion and forgiveness, integrity and wisdom, respect and honesty. You can choose merely to permit God to be in your life. Or you can unlock your peaceful core, and live God from the inside out.

OUR SPIRITUAL BEING

Peace. Whatever method you use to reveal it, whether it is through meditation, a mantra, prayers or prayer beads, yoga, through breathing or even music and dance, the effect is the same. It can also be discovered in a single moment where the body is still, the mind quiet and the wonder of the world around us reveals our underlining spirit, the universal energy of stillness.

That peace buried within each of us, once it is found, it is a life-changing event, and it becomes a force and a focal point for our lives. The real revelation is not that we have deep inner peace within us, but rather, that it has always been there, and it is as much a part of our being as our mind and our body. It is the link that ties us to our world and the universe that is all things, or if you prefer, to God. Experiencing this inner peace, however, is just the starting point. It cannot become the anchor to our spirit or our life without understanding that in all things there is always a relationship. You can think of it as a cycle of energy between all things and that in its natural state it is always in balance.

For peace to become the catalyst that allows us to expand our spirit, we must understand the influences of those relationships that surround us, both the tangible and intangible. Those nuances between each other, our communities, and the world we all share. Identifying and comprehending those relationships enables our mind to start cultivating changes that have positive effects. This requires some effort on our part, to work to find and maintain a balanced between our inner and outer self, between each other, the natural world we live in and even with God. This essentially encompasses our entire ecosphere, and again it all revolves around relationships. With any of these connections, whether it is tangible or intangible, we first need awareness and then a level of respect for each relationship.

Our relationship with each other and the one we all share with our planet are the two foremost of our physical relationships. Discovering or unveiling our inner peace is the basis for understanding some of the intangible relationships. To know that peace is within us, without trying to understand how this conduit connects to everything else gains us little in the way of spiritual insight. Our purpose here is to find our center, that inner peace, and learn to balance our emotions and our daily lives. We then need to find ways to improve not just our own lives but also enhance those relationships within our community and those within our environment. Spiraling out from self we need to respect one another's lives, livelihoods and treat each other equally. To recognize that these same principles also apply to our planet and that we continue to seek equilibrium in all things.

Our goal is not to become devoid of our emotions. They are an integral part of who we are. We do however need to learn how to reel in the extremes, to buffer the raw, instinctive emotions of fear and anger with a conscientious pause. To push aside our impulsive reactions to prevent them from carrying us away, down a path that is damaging to others and ourselves. We cannot help to experience stresses, but we also need to understand its effects on us. We cannot change the fact that our lives are ruled by our emotions, but our course should always be charted by a conscious choice. We must remember that we cannot take back or change the moment that just happened, but we can help determine what happens in the next moment and the ones after that.

Yes, we need our emotions. We also need to let them out, we need to share them, but more importantly, sometimes, we need to let go of them. When venting the worst of them, we should find a way to do so that is non-destructive. This takes us back to our spiritual selves and that inner-peace which is our conduit to the divine. We should, whenever we can, release them into the vast emptiness that is our peaceful core, the God within. One of the great benefits of having that relationship with internal peace is that over time, it will take the hard edge off our stress emotions, allowing us to live a calmer life.

It is also important to understand that our spirit and our body cannot be separated while we are still living. You cannot have the spiritual without the emotional or physical. Trying to disengage from the body or dismissing the spirit defeats our purpose for which we are born, it twists the route we were intended to traverse. Neither were we born into this world to search out some sort of perfection of spirit. Our goal is balance. The peace within is there to help us reach an equilibrium of self then a sense of balance in the relationships between the spiritual and physical realms, our social and environmental circles.

There cannot be peace and harmony in everyday life without giving a little time to the daily practice of experiencing quietness. We stimulate introspection by inwardly cultivating our inner peace, but this thought-provoking state of being is also grounded in outwardly embracing equality and respect. This again leads us back to our relationships and seeking a balance in them. When we are done looking inward, we should again look outward. Once awakened, we cannot just wait for others to wake up to their spirituality. We cannot be passive. We have a purpose; it is found in our inherent ability to nurture and to guide. We have to teach everyone.

Some might say that ultimately the only things we can change are ourselves, but our own personal journey of change is just the beginning, not the end. Once we find inner-peace, we need to open our eyes and look upon the world again, to respect it and try to understand the relationship we see there and then try to propagate positive changes in the wider world. Our life-long vision should be to leave nature and our society in a better state than when we entered it. Even if it is through one tiny ripple at a time. This is the full interpretation of our spiritual journey. By living this way are we not also fulfilling those expectations that God has for us.

Again, you can call it peace or the presence of God or the conscious living universe, but it is all the same. It does not require mystical incantations, mind-altering compounds, or body-altering processes to achieve an understanding of inner peace. Paired with the two mandates of equality and the sanctity of life, this peace becomes an inner strength, and this gives us the ability to push changes in our world. Spirituality without a sense of responsibility to your community, our environment, and the future of both, does not elevate our soul.

Our strengths come from body, mind, and spirit. Knowing when to draw your strength from the right source is essential. When the body and the mind are tired or weakened, we can reach inward and understand that the peace within is always there, we can draw our strength from the spirit through that conduit that connects us to the world and the universe.

Again, once you uncover the peace within, you know it, for it alters your state of being. The awareness of inner peace is not something we continuously need work to hold on to, because it is built-in. Even in the briefest of moments during a day, you can find it and know it is always there when you need it, to give you strength for your fully engaged journey through all the circles of life.

Our spiritual journey through life, through the physical world, is not about self and it is not merely about a personal search for enlightenment or nirvana or heaven. To a certain extent, this path is to prepare us for our next state of being, but we are not born to learn how to die. Life is meant to be lived and experienced. We have a path we were tasked to complete, that journey encompasses all of our interactions throughout our lives, the ones we have with each other, with the world around us, and with God.

Living in isolation, praying and meditating to try to disconnect from all the circles of life, is a fruitless attempt towards purification of spirit. We cannot further clarify our core because the peace within is already a part of us, and it is already pure. We can only embrace it and allow it to help propagate positive changes which can improve the way we live. This is even more meaningful when we continue to stay fully connected to the rest of our world.

A spirituality built on the idea of only looking inward is a false path. It often becomes the domain of the few since it is seen as only obtainable by the enlightened. Exclusion and isolation from the rest of society often become the norm. The tenets behind this spiritual ideal seem to imply that a higher level of conscious illumination is just not obtainable by the untrained, or uninitiated because it is thought to be out of reach, to the weak minds of the everyday person. This is not the case. Inner peace applies equally to everyone.

When we look at spirituality in its entirety, it is not about a personal journey, it is about relationships. It is always looking around, being aware of each circle of life, sensing the exchange of energy through all those relationships, and learning to live and coexist within them.

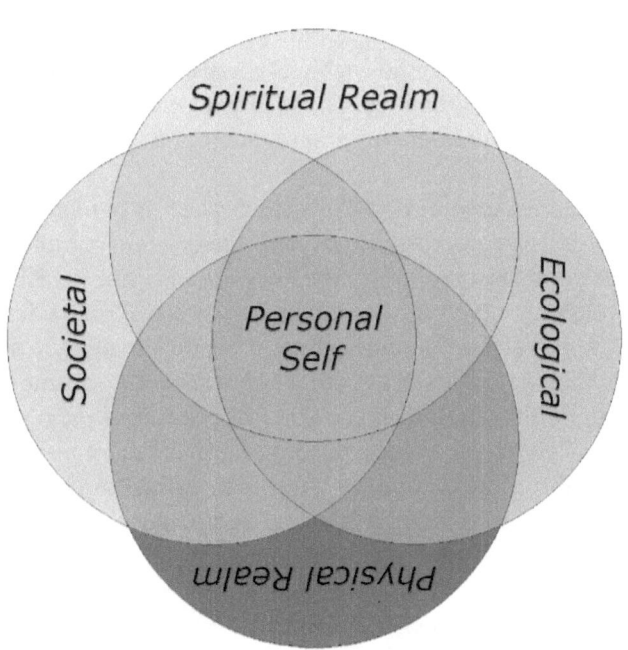

The Heart of Community

What is the heart of any society? It has its roots in family and the extended family, but a community is more than that. On a broader scale, it is about people living together, supporting and help each other, and in turn enabling the entire group to thrive. It includes safeguarding the entire group, but it is also about an expectation of each individual's acceptable behavior. Ideally, the heart of the community is treating each other respectfully with a full measure of fairness. Those traditions of conduct likely stemmed directly from some of our primitive and instinctive natures, that of protecting, nurturing and then guidance. These follow closely in line behind our most primary natures of self-preservation and procreation.

Day to day survival was likely the first priority of early humankind. Roles within a group may not have been completely gender-based but situational. Proficiency in different skillsets would have weighed more heavily on an individual's role because the group's survival was dependent on the efficient use of each person's individual talents. As groups of humankind became successful and grew in size, larger societies where formed. Only then did roles and tradition gradually become hard set as morals and even laws. At least this was so by the dawn of civilization. So, what then, is central to defining the heart of a society or a community? The answer is Harmony.

But this has been very hard to come by in most cultures around the world throughout history. We have been driven apart by so many factors because we have a habit of overlooking or ignoring what we should be doing to enrich our communities. Some of our biggest faults here are caused by a culture of persistent inequality. The most basic and pervasive is the one between men and women. Alternatives variants or misinterpreted version of what is considered a truth are also problematic when trying to finding harmony in our societies. Traditions, religions and even governments can create some of the most challenging roadblocks that can obstruct the evolution of the human spirit within a community or a country. However, sometimes these institutions can also become very good at driving change that enhances it.

The first of these divisive elements can be defined by the absents of equality and respect. It is not the color of our skin or our sex that separates us and drives out harmony. It is not even our various cultures or religions that divide us, nor is it the difference between the level of our knowledge. What ultimately sets us apart is our attitude towards each other. It is the actions that we take and direction those actions take us. We unleashed it with the injustices that are committed against our neighbor which can fuel a situation to escalate out of control and is intensified by the sheer cruelty of our words and deeds on both sided of the conflict. This is what cut deepest into the very soul of our humanity. This is what drives the wedge between us and where does that leave us...wanting or seeking vengeance? Much of this is perpetuated and defined by a self-proclaim or even a presumed God-given right of entitlement. A hierarchy where some people inherently are of greater value and others have less or no value in society. This kind of disparity is the divisive element that drives out harmony and even stifles peace.

It is our arrogance our ignorance, our intolerance that prevents us from seeing the depth of our own faults or the deep moral debt, which is tied to our mortal hypocrisies. God in the form of peace requires us to respect one another and treat each other equally. For us to put aside our hate, to let it go. To pause and let our anger subside for a brief moment which then allows us to look around and reflect. Can you not see the suffering? Is your heart so hardened by hateful bigotry, inflammatory religious indignation, inflexible customs, and traditions or the unjustified fear of the unfamiliar that you cannot allow compassion to enter your hearts? How we treated others throughout our life is a reflection on how we will be treated by God at the end of our journey.

The second of these divisive elements is found in our lack of awareness, understanding or in the outright denial of truth. In the physical world, the one truth is that everything is governed and held together by an endless myriad of intertwined relationships. From the moment we are conceived we have been bound to those relationships. In nature, there are no illusions except for those connections we overlook, choose to ignore or do not comprehend. How one perceives the physical world is purely a matter of perspective and understanding.

A tree may perceive the soil, the air, the water in both and maybe even gravity. A squirrel in this tree has a different perspective of the tree, but it is still the same reality, the same tree. This is the same for the person standing under the tree looking at the squirrel and the hawk in the sky eyeing the same squirrel. Two very different perspectives but still only one universe. The reality in the physical world is the same whether it is from the squirrel, hawk or human's standpoint. We were born in this one reality and are connected to the myriad of relationships that exist and define our universe.

Truth, when viewed from within these relationships whether it's between each other or nature is sometimes harder to define. Truth within our social and environmental circles is not just based on right or wrong but is also determined by our perception of something. Viewing something or someone from only one angle or perspective does not often reveal a truth. So too, a lack of awareness or understanding of something, or an individual and any of the actions associated with these can lead us to a conclusion that we have observed a truth, when in fact, we may not have.

Observation and clarification are the basic building blocks in determining a truth. This requires endless curiosity and expanded discoveries to elevate our logic and reasoning. This level of scrutiny about a given association will ultimately define it as a confirmed truth or prove it wrong. Relationships in the natural world can be determined through this process of continually seeking better answers. But this does not always translate when we start looking at our social circles. Truth in this circle of life can often become a much more complex process.

Here truth comes in various shades of gray. In our environmental circle, the truth is limited to how much we comprehend the world around us. Truth within our social circle can be even more vague. It could be defined as knowing a right from a wrong, observing what is and what is not accurate or merely sensing or reasoning that the logic about something is off then pursuing the right answers. But, there are also other factors involved. Ignorance and arrogance can serve up their own twisted form of a so-called truth, as can hate, fear, and anger. Self-righteousness and many other human emotions and values can create an illusion of truth to justify a necessity or an ideology.

Generally, this is because we are only willing to accept our own version of what we believe is a truth even if it is proven false. These are perceived as such by those willing to accept it as true but not necessarily understand its underlying nature or even the ramification it has on others or ourselves, or how their version of that truth affects the present or our future. We proclaim a rationale as a certainty and then balk when it cannot be equally applied to different situations, in reverse, or in regards to the sanctity of another person's life.

Truth is often hard to distinguish. Most will find it in the things they want to believe in, but the truth can always be found in the bedrock and the living soil of our lives. It emanates from peace and harmony, equality and respect, love and honesty, integrity and wisdom. Truth is the wild rose that grows out of these virtues and stands firm against the elements, against all the deceitful things we are willing to or are led to believe. These forms of deception like winter can force their harshness on truth and make it appear to be dead, but since truth is a product of those virtues, that living soil, it will continue in the hearts of those who embrace these values, to regrow and bloom with spring's inevitable arrival.

The third of these divisive elements is found at the governing level of society, in the traditions and doctrines of the various political and religious organizations. Today, countries are often made up of many provinces and hundreds or thousands of communities that are often tied together by ethnic groups, religions, or other social factions. Even at these higher levels of society, the heart of it, its mission has not changed much. It should still be about supporting and helping each other, safeguarding people's lives and property, providing laws that guarantee those people's rights and to ensure that everyone is treated fairly.

The central role here should still be harmony, but the scope is much broader. A government should be providing a clear sense of overall identity, yet continue to maintain equality and opportunity. Its purpose is even more critical if there are widely diverse people spread throughout many regions. A government should also be providing protections for our environment so that the next generation does not suffer physically, emotionally, or monetarily from the greed of the previous ones.

A society or government that does not treat everyone fairly or equally is quite likely, being similarly disrespectful to their environment. So, the heart of our broader sense of community is both respect and harmony, between its people and with nature. These are also two of the most basic building blocks of a healthy relationship. This again is a reflection of the most fundamental reality in the universe, which is, it is made up of endless connections. Relationships that need to be nurtured and respected.

In all matters, the leaders who we have chosen to manage our governmental and religious institutions must remember that they are there to serve and to be role models to their constituents. All of them regardless of their political party or religious organization should be actively looking for ways to enhance our societies. They should be impartial in the position, neither accepting nor courting favors or giving any special favors. They should listen first to their people, all the people, and put self-interest aside. Neither should they propagate anger, fear, or hate but rather promote unity and harmony. They should speak calmly, be patient, and be firm in their resolve to serve the will of the people and to do this with wisdom and integrity. To help create laws for the people, but also to protect the land that provides for the needs for all of humanity. This should be done not just for the people of today but for the welfare of people and the environment for all generations to come.

Fixing our current problems will require us to correct the most fundamental issues since the formation of civilization, that of equality, full equal rights, and a higher level of respect toward each other. In prehistoric times when death was a day-to-day reality, survival depended on each person in their family or group doing their part. Everyone found or learned a skillset, and this provided a depth of strength and fortitude to the larger group. Those skills, regardless of whether they were mastered by a male or a female were critical when dealing with an often-unforgiving world.

As we face the problems of our own time, we need to return to that ideal, where the best-suited skillset of each individual is encouraged regardless of whether they are male or female. More than ever, our best minds are needed to find solutions to our social and environmental issues. Addressing the fundamental inequality between men and women is a good first step, and this will take us a long way in tackling all the other biases that are holding humanity back from real social evolution.

Very simply put, we need to look back on the nature of the physical world to better understand how it should be within the working of our social and ecological circles. In the physical world, everything is bound and governed by relationships. As we then look at the nature of the relationships around us, we realize that there is a free-flowing exchange of energy, a cycle of give and take between everything and everyone. There has to exist a balance in those exchanges, an equilibrium within each relationship because each is interdependent on the other, whether it is perceived or not. The energy that is received through those relationships becomes the energy released, though the outward form it takes will likely be very different. The physical world dictates many types of balances. Just as our societal and ecological circles inject their own unique but equally important demands for balance.

Finding equilibrium in our social circle means treating each other equally and protecting the sanctity of life inside and outside of our groups. In our environmental circle, this means protecting the balance in nature by finding ways to harvest what we need but also to return what we do not need, that being our waste, back to our environment in a form that can benefit nature and not degrade it. We cannot find peace if there is an absence of harmony. When there is not equality for all, respect and honesty are easier to overlook. What is love without nurturing and guidance. Without any of these principles, integrity, and wisdom will be short-lived. What is humanity without the inspiration, the desire, the reasoning, and the logic to unlocking the true heart of community.

The Soul of Nature

Nature is not meant to be worshipped, though it must be respected. It is part of our life's blood, and we are a part of it. That means that a truly balanced lifestyle must include achieving harmony with nature. We must remember that we are embedded in our ecosphere no matter how far removed we think we are from it. What harms the environment will eventually affect our health and well-being. Nature has a vitality and spirit though different from our own, and this needs to be recognized, looked after, and cared for just like the relationship we have with each other or even God.

This means we should not over-exploit the environment whether it is plant or animal, the land or the ocean. Learning to take a balanced and conscientious approach to what is acquired from the land or the sea will help maintain its health and vitality from generation to generation. But since this is a relationship, one based on a cycle of energy between the two, we also need to look at what we give back to our environment. How we give our waste back is critical. What we give back should be in a form that enhances nature, not destroys or poisons the land, the water and the living things that inhabit those environments.

We must do better in this, to find ways to transform our waste, both human and industrial because it is a matter of life and death for our earth and ultimately for us. Our lives are dependent on the air, land, and oceans. The general well-being of those three really does have a direct bearing on our health. Respect for the environment should be as ingrained in us as our inborn desire to love and care for our children.

The earth, as in its biosphere has a presence; it has a spirit and a soul because it is full of life. We are a part of it because we are in a relationship with it whether we live in the country or in an urban setting. We are physically part of our environment, and indeed we are even tied to it spiritually. Our environment not only has effects on our health, but it can also have an impact on our mood and our emotions. Nature sustains us in a multitude of ways and on many different levels, and when the relationship we share with it is exploitive, we ultimately end up hurt ourselves in that process.

Let us back up for a moment here and clarify one thing. At its worst, nature can be harsh, unforgiving and cruel, which is not unlike people sometimes. But whereas people are capable of acts of kindness, nature generally gives no mercy. Nature at its best is our ultimate provider. All of our physical needs can be supplied by its wealth of diverse resources. From food and healing plants to the raw materials needed to enhance our daily lives. It also has a hidden side, that if we are open to it, can open our minds, our heart, our soul to a deep sense of peace. It can help open that door to our own inner peace.

Humankind at its worst can be toxic free radicals, a cancer, a poison and the most systematic exploiters of the land and the oceans. At our best, we can be a medicine that can start the healing process that can enhance and protect our biosphere. The land and the oceans are a living entity, full of life and they are currently in need of healing, of both physical and spiritual. The land, the sea, and even the air should be just as precious to us as our families, our children and our faith in God. Environmental harmony is obtained through our balanced relationship with it. This is about synergy, collaborations, interactions, cooperation, recycling, conservation and that cycle of energy between the two.

How can we have any vision of our future if our eyes and lungs burn from our toxic air? How can our families grow healthy roots when our soil and the groundwater are polluted by the chemicals we carelessly use and throw away every day? When will we learn that our health is dependent on the well-being of our environment? We often do not realize that our spiritual well-being is also tied to this underlying harmony between ourselves and all of nature. That we will not find complete oneness without this balanced relationship, and this requires us to keep the world around us healthy.

A poisoned world leads to a poisoning of all life on this planet. We cannot run from it, we cannot hide, and we cannot quickly move away from those problems. One country cannot be better at conservation then another because what affects one, affects others. We do have a fundamental problem with our attitude towards nature and our waste. In the greater scheme of things, it is not the problem that defines a situation, it is our approach to those issues that makes all the difference. Indifference and denial solve nothing.

At this point, we also need to look at another definition of the word waste. Humankind is also the biggest waster of our planet's resources because we generally do not make things to last or in most cases, even try to build things that can stand up against the forces of nature. We choose the less expensive or the easiest solution. Waste in the form of low-quality products is the direct result of the profit mongers that plague our societies. Cheap and low-quality means products will be thrown out sooner, which means it generates additional sales and then higher profits for companies that have no concern or vision of the future beyond their own profit margins. We build what could be considered cardboard houses and live in a throwaway world. When the big storms in our lives come along, which are an eventuality, and they destroy all of these things, we are devastated. Not only does this cause hardship and heartache to those affected but the sheer volume of waste and pollution those events generate is enormous. The impact of which is waste on a multitude of levels and this has a far-reaching consequence for ourselves and our environment. Yet, this is also the result of our own shortsightedness, greed, and laziness.

When it comes to the things that are most important to us, our homes, our communities, and the infrastructure that supports these, it seems we are more likely to take the least expensive solution. The lowest bid philosophy is just wasteful if it leads to poorly constructed buildings whether they are homes or other structures. We need to look at each local environment we live in and build it to withstand the worst that nature can throw at those communities.

Everything that goes into our construction projects should be of the highest quality with the longest lifespan possible. Everything we build should stand up to the day to day use of many years. This philosophy also should include all the large and small items in which we fill our homes and workspaces. Our homes should also be designed to be inhabitable for generations and to stand the tests of time with minimal amounts of regular maintenance.

Managing our waste is not just about achieving a clean environment. Everything should be made to be recycled or be returned to nature in a way that enhances our environment. Re-use and recycle is not enough even if we can reach a point where 100% of our waste is managed that way. We also cannot be wasteful with the resources we have left in the first place. Products with longer lifespans are replaced less often, and this can reduce the overall waste we generate, and when we create less, we have less of it to manage. More efficient construction and manufacturing methods can reduce waste in two ways. Less damage when disaster strikes mean less waste that needs to be cleaned up afterward. Less damage also means less rebuilding which reduces any further strain on both our natural and financial resources.

There is a kinship with the land, the sea, and all of the creatures that roam above, on and under the two. With our environment, we must side with caution and not for selfish profit or sheer ignorance. The revenue, the wealth gained today at the expense of our environment, will have an exponentially higher return of debt for those in the future to repair the damage. A healthy landscape means a balanced relationship with it and in turn a healthy lifestyle for us, which then can help us create harmony between the body, the mind, and the spirit.

Walking Out of the Dark: Part Three

Storm of Confusion

Troubled thoughts flash on the horizon, distant lightning heralds the coming of a storm that drifts across the mind's sky.

Confusion in the gloom of the gathering clouds, gently it falls with the first soft drops of rain, blurring the graying horizon.

Worry quickens the rain, the wind pushes it into giant slanting sheets, drenching everything to its very soul.

Terror leaps down, bolts of electricity splitting the air with bright flashes, reoccurring with such ferocity that the clouds glow an eerie green.

Fear and helplessness bring the hail, it pounds out its fury, laying low all in its path, thunder proclaiming its victory.

Numbness comes in the night, the dark at its very bleakest, as the rains cease, there is an unsettling stillness in the silence.

Dreams and ideas twisted by the whirling winds, the roar of the cyclone pulls all into its center, the vortex rips and shreds then flings it aside.

Exhaustion brings a calming of the storm, the winds die, the thunder fades, and the rain eases into a soft spring shower, bringing with it a rebirth and new life.

Fresh thoughts form in the lingering mist, light gray the morning fog, with its hushed and muted sounds, there is a pressure to its presence.

Love and trust glow through the mist, the distant sun heats the air, the fog melts away to reveal a bright new day.

With squinting eyes, comes the comprehension of the vastness of the mind's sky and many new and shining horizons.

During the war, Arthur spent all of his time fighting with the Revolutionary Army as an irregular. Only after the civil war was over did Arthur think about returning to the university to finish his education. Throughout the conflict, Arthur had looked for the field marshal, but their paths never crossed again. Even after the war, he was never able to find out what happened to him. The idea of that evil man living free somewhere troubled Arthur deeply.

After earning his degree, Arthur decided to stay in the capital. He worked at several jobs created by the new government, but the more things changed, the more they remained the same. After five years, he had grown angry and frustrated. He had been overworked and, more pointedly, felt overlooked. He had applied for promotions more times than he could count. Yet it seemed that he just did not have the right connections within the regular army, which influenced almost everything in the city. What troubled him most was the fact that he was never honestly considered for those promotions, even though he felt he had been the strongest candidate for some of those jobs. Through those years, he had also grown weary of the city life and all the politics. Nonetheless, despite the lack of promotions, the money was decent.

He had not been the same person since those horrible days just before the revolution. That hardship, coupled with several failed relationships, had left him teetering on the edge of hopelessness, heartbroken, and at times deeply depressed. He was also beginning to feel that he was somehow letting his mum down as well as his aunt and uncle. They had worked hard to give him the opportunity to do something better in his life, but so far, he just didn't feel he was living up to that expectation. His life seemed shallow and unfulfilled, and happiness felt like only a memory.

The letters to his aunt and, even more importantly, to Mairwyn were getting harder and harder for him to write. The words did not flow as freely as they used to, and the letters were fewer and farther between. All of this weighed heavily on his mind. He knew he needed to make changes in his life, but he was not sure how or even what needed changing.

When the winds of change finally blew in, they came on suddenly, with a force that sent him spinning. Like so many times in his past, what disturbed him most were the recurring dreams—the ones with vague flashes of memories of his parents. They always seemed to resurface just before bad events played out in his life. Even more unsettling was that they included even more vivid recollections of his uncle. He too was playing a part in those morning storms of dreams and memories.

After these vivid morning dreams started, he decided it was time for him to leave the capital and go home, back to the inn and his aunt. He had been avoiding going back, but now it seemed the right thing to do, and once he had decided what to do, a new urgency kicked in. It seemed he could not make all the necessary arrangements fast enough. When the day finally came for him to start his journey home, he did not hesitate, and he did not look back.

When Arthur finally arrived at the inn, Olena greeted him from behind the front desk. "*Arthur!*" she yelled as she ran around the counter to give him a big hug. *For someone who looks so frail*, Arthur thought, *she sure gave a mighty big hug*.

"You look so…so… Well, you've grown into a fine man. But you look a little too skinny to me," she said in a teasing voice. "You need to eat better. Come; your aunt will be so happy to see you." She started to walk toward the back apartment that was his aunt's home and then stopped and turned toward Arthur. "She has not been well lately, Arthur, and I have been worried sick about her. Having you home again will be very good for her, I think. Very good indeed."

When Arthur walked into his aunt's bedroom, his heart sank. Kaisa was propped up in bed reading a book, but she looked so very pale and much frailer than even Olena. When she finally looked up, she started to cry.

"Oh, Arthur my boy, I am so delighted to see you. Come. Sit," she said as she patted a spot on the bed next to her. As quickly as he sat down, she leaned forward and wrapped her arms around him, and they hugged for a time. "I love you," she said softly in his ear. "I love you like you were my own, and I always knew you would find your way back. You have always had a knack for showing up when you are needed the most."

They talked for more than an hour catching up. They touched on a wide range of topics, except one—the matter of what was ailing his aunt—and Arthur was reluctant to ask. Eventually, she did get around to talking about it. She told him that she had cancer, and her remaining time was short. Arthur could no longer keep his bottled-up emotion in check and started to weep. More than ever, he wanted and needed to be home, surrounded by the people he loved. He had hoped that coming home would help him find a way out of the darkness he felt inside. That it could start him down a path to feeling whole again.

Yet again, it seemed that those hurricanes of dreams and memories foretold another tragedy in his life. That he would soon be saying his final goodbye and bury another loved one. It was too much to keep inside, and he began telling his aunt about the dawn cloudbursts of memories and emotions that always seemed to be forewarnings of bad things to come. He also talked for the first time about the atrocities he had seen and experienced before and during the revolution. He even told her he felt that he had failed his mum and, more importantly, her and his uncle.

"Oh, Arthur, you have not let me down yet, nor could you ever, and I can tell you that you did not let your uncle down or, for that matter, your mum either." She reached out, put her hand on his cheek, and looked him in the eyes. "It saddens me to hear of the great turmoil you have had to live through, but it seems to me that you may be looking at certain things from the wrong perspective. Maybe God was speaking to you through the memories of your mum—warning you, yes, but also telling you that you were needed and that you had a part to play."

Arthur stiffened, but Kaisa went on softly. "Please, Arthur, let me finish. I don't think they were harbingers of bad things. You said those memories woke you up early on the day my Zachary died. Now stop and think about what could have happened if you had not gotten up early that morning. There is another thing you may not have realized. That old man in the jail cell—the one that you say saved your life; the one you sent to me with your message—that journey for him became a turning point in his life."

"And now I am here to help you again," Arthur replied.

"Maybe," she said. "Or maybe there are other people here who need you more than I do. I would like you to consider doing two favors for me, but I will get to that in a minute. First, I have a bit of a confession to make. Before your mum died, she made me promise to send you to the university. I did not agree, and we argued horribly about it—but in the end, I reluctantly promised to make sure it happened. She wanted so badly for you to find a better life, and I had so many reservations about her plans. I almost did not live up to that promise, Arthur. Forgive me for not telling you about your mum's plan sooner. It would have given you time to better prepare yourself for that huge change."

"I most certainly forgive you," said Arthur, "and I think you may have been right about those misgivings. Sending me down to the capital to attend the university hasn't led to any great successes for me."

"Only time will tell, Arthur; only time knows the true destination of any journey in your life," she said. "Now, about those two favors, I would like you to do. First, Mathias really needs to talk to you. He has something he needs to discuss with you."

"Who is Mathias?" asked Arthur.

"I think you only knew him as Philthy. He lives and helps over at the brickworks. I could never persuade him to stay in one of the rooms at the inn. Stubborn old coot, he is."

"And the second favor?" asked Arthur. He had a feeling about what she was going to say before she said anything, and he was right.

"Mairwyn," she said. "I don't know where she may be at this time of the morning, but don't delay in finding her. She plans to leave the inn first thing in the morning. Now, my dear boy, I need my rest. If all else fails, you might be able to find Mairwyn on the roof at sunset. She is often up there at that time of day, but Mathias will at the brickworks all day."

Arthur gave his aunt one more hug and left her to rest.

Section 4

A Recipe for Living

Good chefs value the quality of their ingredients and see this as an indicator of potential. In our own diet, we should do the same. With our food, we need to evaluate its quality, how natural or how processed it is. Being mindful of the wholesomeness of the ingredients we keep in our pantry is a good habit to start. We can then choose those least processed to create a healthier lifestyle.

In many ways, the emotions we express are like the ingredients in the food we eat. They can be sweet, sour, spicy, or bitter. Within our day-to-day life, how we act, interact, and react becomes part of our own recipe for living. It is like when you carefully measure the correct proportions of flour, honey, cinnamon, salt, and other ingredients to make something good to eat. However, without moderation, without the right mix of favors, those individual ingredients in our cooking can make the final product overpowering, unappetizing, or inedible. The best recipe for our life is following the simplest of truths in how we express ourselves, how we handle the situations we find ourselves in, and how we learn to cope.

Our soul needs a good chef as well; however, we alone are our own sous-chef. As such, we need to evaluate the quality of our own character before confronting and overcoming the turmoil in our lives. Balancing our lives and our emotions through the peace at our core is the first step. Unlike cooking, though, it is not how we use our emotions but how we handle and manage them that creates a healthier lifestyle and contributes to our well-being.

The Simplest of Truths

In our daily life, we can often become overwhelmed by our emotions, and these ingredients impart a flavor to the relationships around us. We can experience sadness, hurt and pain, anger, fear, and even happiness, but in the wrong proportions, they can cause an imbalance in our lives. Honestly weighing our experiences, good or bad, and then learning from them creates a better life for us. We cannot always control the things that affect our lives or pull on our emotions but left unchecked, they can imbue an essence in our lives that can become domineering, unappealing, and unpleasant. When our recipe includes the simplest of truths, we can use the ingredients that we have on hand and transform them by evaluating, adjusting, and processing them by a holistic approach to create something that not only produces clarity and harmony but also enriches our soul.

The Peace Within

The deep peace that exists within each of us is not always found on our own; instead, it is sometimes revealed in very unassuming ways. Any of us can experience moments where a deeply peaceful feeling basically washes over us. These obscure and reflective moments can quiet the mind, which in turn illuminates a path. For those who have perceived it, they may even have experienced an epiphany. Yet so often, those revelations are left unexplored. We easily overlook or dismiss them and fail to recognize the possibilities. Still, those passageways are always there. Our own route to that inner peace often remains abstract and hard to uncover.

A more consistent and reliable avenue can be discovered or revealed through prayer and meditation. Prayer is about talking to God, and meditation is about listening. When woven together, they can help us uncover our own path to our peaceful core. Before you start this process, consider a type of prayer or a set of prayers that suits you and memorize it or them. Find a spot that is quiet and comfortable. Depending on where you are, and if it is safe, light a candle and place it a short distance away. The flame of a candle becomes a focal point to keep parts of your mind busy. Using prayer beads can also help by keeping your body and a portion of your conscious mind occupied. Both are worthy options and an excellent way to start.

Pray, and repeat the cycle of prayers as many times as you feel comfortable. Let the words of your prayers keep your conscious mind busy. Your mind will want to swim in an endless river of random thoughts but pay no attention to them. As ideas and thoughts move in, do not contemplate them, do not ask why, and do not let them hold your attention. Instead, let them drift by, release them, and keep praying.

The Simplest of Truths

Close your eyes and look deep into yourself. Look past the prayer you are praying and past the random firings of thoughts. Move through them, under them, around them, and beyond them, until they become no more than a constant chatter. Move your mind away from that noise, and keep praying until those prayers feel like nothing more than someone else talking off in the distance.

Eventually, you may feel as if time is slowing; sense the motionlessness as time seems to stop. Let your mind gaze into the stillness; touch it with your soul. Sense serenity, for it is bliss; it is peace. Embrace the timeless quiet, for this peace, is the real core of your being; it is God.

Look into the stillness and let go of your resentment, your sorrow, and your pain. Release it. Let your fear, your hate, and your anger subside. Feel the heaviness of those burdens lift off your chest like a bird taking flight, and let it fly away from you into the emptiness. Look again into the stillness and ask for forgiveness. As the peace washes over and through you, let it inundate your soul. If you feel the need to cry, do not hold it in, and just allow it to happen.

Return to the stillness and give thanks. Seek the tranquility, ask for help, and then let go of those intentions and aspirations. Let them be absorbed in the quietness and be patient. Embrace and live by the simplest of truths, trust yourself and the peace within, and you will know in your heart the right path to take and be confident in the choices you must make every day. Never forget to draw your strength from the deep peace that dwells within. Remember every day and always that all things lay within us, and peace is our epicenter.

Both Sides of the Coin

To say, that a coin has two sides can metaphorically mean many different things, but for the moment, this concept will be limited to currency and wealth. If you ask anyone to define currency, most would immediately say it is money. Others might interpret it as an exchange where goods or services are bartered for a needed item or other services. The negotiated medium of exchange becomes the currency in a transaction between a buyer and seller.

One could say that a coin not only represents the monetary value of an exchange but also both contingents of that transaction. Each side of the coin is a promise for the realization of a need or a desire for both parties. Therefore, the raw potential within the negotiated transaction—or, more simply put, the agreement between two parties—can be represented as one type of coin we will call the Coin of Opportunity.

Not so long ago, we lived mostly in a wealth-based economy. This meant people only used their accumulated wealth, whether that was money or surplus goods, to purchase or trade for something new, and you had to have some form of wealth or marketable skill before any barter could take place. For those lacking resources, taking on debt was one way to provide for a need or, hopefully, try to build success. Unfortunately, this often left those people open to the risk of exploitation.

Today we are faced with an economy that is mostly debt-driven. This is not just determined by the demand for debt but by our need or desire to obtain things that are beyond our means. It is also encouraged by a for-profit fulfillment of that demand for debt. This is often weighed heavily against those who take on the debt. It may even be promoted as a simple business transaction. But, because of hidden fees and obscure clauses, contracts may not always be easy to understand. In most parts of the world today, there are laws to protect lenders and borrowers. But this can still leave people of lesser means at risk.

Regardless of what side of any transaction you are on, merely having the Coin of Opportunity is not enough in life. When faced with the prospects this coin provides, we need to become accountable for ourselves and assume a responsible attitude toward making a profit and/or taking on debt. Before borrowing money, we should consider the amount of money we earn, how we earn our money versus why we decide to borrow money, the amount of that debt, and the terms of that agreement. Therefore, effectively balancing our income/profits and our debts—or, more simply put, balancing our needs versus our desires—can represent another coin we will call the Coin of Responsibility.

Being successful in our transactions, directly or indirectly, often builds wealth. Each success provides access to even better opportunities. As our wealth increases, so should our responsibility to do something more significant with it. Despite our individual level of wealth, however, we all have the capacity to pass along the Coin of Opportunity, which can actually take on many different forms. When we do this, we expect the coin to be received with the understanding that it is not lightly given.

By accepting the Coin of Opportunity, we also need to reach for the Coin of Responsibility, but this coin cannot be given—this coin must be earned through our own efforts. To squander an opportunity and gain nothing long-lasting from it leaves both sides unfulfilled and could set a precedent where fewer opportunities arise.

These two coins are still not enough, because there is a higher moral responsibility than just how we utilize our opportunities, acquire wealth, and manage our debt. Again, regardless of which side of the transaction you represent, we all need to approach each other with respect and honesty. Ultimately, our success or failure depends on a level of integrity and mutual trust from both sides.

In the greater scheme of life, we must look beyond our worldly wealth because ultimately, it is of very little consequence. What is important is whether we have been fair and responsible while gaining our wealth or paying off our debts. That we provided the opportunities that allowed others to build their own success. Hopefully, in that process, we also helped them grow to their fullest potential. Therefore, the opportunities we respectfully receive and honorably pass along—or, more simply put, the integrity within our daily exchanges—can represent a third coin we will call the Coin of Conscience.

There is one more thing we need to consider about currency, and this pushes us past our financial transactions. Here we must dive deeper into our personal interactions, for there is more to consider than the face value of the currency in our daily exchanges with each other.

We can also use the coin to describe parts of ourselves—one face being how we allow others to perceive us and the other is our true self. The images on both sides of this coin are based on the integrity of our everyday interactions and relationships. This relates not only to how we manage ourselves in each of our transactions but also in our personal relationships with family, friends, and society in general. It is about how our actions affect others. The question is, do we perceive or even comprehend our true self? Do we even care about the differences on each side of that coin?

On its own, the Coin of Opportunity can send us down many different paths in life. Not all are the right paths to follow. In our human quest for fulfillment, it is not only our desire for more that can get us in trouble but the desire to fulfill our needs as effortlessly as possible that puts us at the most significant social, moral, and divine risk. There is nothing wrong with wanting more from life, so long as you pursue that end honestly, and it does not come at the unfair expense of anyone else. The exploitation of anyone solely for your own benefit is a direct result of the worst type of uncaring and callous attitude, and this goes against the very nature of the simplest of truths. More importantly, it goes against God. These actions are personal burdens that weigh on our soul. They are our spiritual debt, our ugliness.

When we start placing a higher value on our actions and the consequences of those activities, we can then begin to visualize our spiritual ugliness but also recognize its beauty. By embracing this type of measured awareness, we start to experience a different kind of fulfillment. Changing the way we think about our day-to-day actions affects the course of our lives. Better decisions lead to better outcomes for you and those around you, and through that, we can gain wisdom. Therefore, the measured awareness of our spiritual beauty versus our spiritual ugliness—or more simply put, our actions and their effects—can be represented by one final coin we will call the Coin of Perception.

So what is it that truly matters in life? It is that we graciously accept the Coin of Opportunity, that we earn the Coin of Responsibility, that we unselfishly acquire the Coin of Conscience, and, through our own introspection, obtain the Coin of Perception. Eventually, a time will come when we have to stand and be judged for our actions. So ask yourselves this: How many coins will I be holding when that time comes? Your real wealth will be measured by the weight of these few coins.

The Conversation

By definition, a conversation requires a minimum of at least two people, but it cannot be considered conversation unless someone is listening and then responds. Life is about how we act and react within all of our worldly relationships, but living is about our conversations, that cycle of energy between the two.

Every relationship starts as a dialogue, and the nature of a quality exchange should ebb and flow freely but cordially. This can spark a conversation that, depending on the course of that exchange, has the potential of leading to a friendship and, possibly, a more meaningful relationship. In musical terms, the conversation revolves around the rhythm and the tone, and our relationship forms around the harmony. Every successful connection is built from the continuation of that initial dialogue, and the ongoing conversation drives the discovery process.

Discovery is and should be a continuous process within any relationship. It helps us navigate the many meandering paths our relationships can take. It also keeps us grounded and moving forward with all of our acquaintances. As any relationship progresses, the discovery process should be weeding out those individuals who may be toxic to our own well-being. Without balance and harmony in our exchanges, a relationship can quickly degrade. When the symmetry in our conversation is lost, the relationship starts to become one-sided. Once in motion, unbalanced or lopsided relationships tend to develop control issues.

These are the types of relationships that we need to recognize as unhealthy and break off because, over time, they can continue to degrade and can very easily slip into abuse. Once it reaches this point, the conversation has likely died and been replaced with what may be nothing more than a series of assumptions, assertions, or orders. There is no conversation in these types of comments because they only move in a single direction. Without free-flowing communication, the relationship will eventually fall apart.

Within our own family bonds, meaning the love we share with our parents and our siblings, certain things are a given and are often implied without words. Friendships and other non-family relationships work from their own set of negotiated dynamics, but we all look for connections and commonality of spirit. We seek to find a point of compatibility and comfort in others. We all search for a level of companionship. Through the sharing of our thoughts and ideas, our feelings and our dreams, the time we spend together can spark those connections.

At some point, whether it is through our own desire and intention or from social or family pressure, we may get married to formalize the bond of our deepest relationship. In doing so, we try to reinforce its successful longevity. Marriage should be about the relationship with your true partner; the one we feel could be our soul mate. This is as opposed to the negotiated transaction of an arranged marriage. This type of agreement suggests a level of ownership over one or both of the persons getting married. As such, it should not be considered an authentic relationship because one may never really blossom. That is not to say a couple cannot build a strong bond this way, but it is a more difficult path to happiness.

Most societies and cultures look at the commitment of marriage as a legal or sacred obligation. One that most people see as a security device, a lock and key that attempts to guarantee that the union will stand the test of time. Yet this agreement or covenant, in and of itself, cannot ensure happiness or even success. That is because marriage is not merely a contract. It is a relationship between two people. Ultimately, the relationship even within the framework of a marriage does not change. It is and should always be considered an external relationship. As such, it relies on the conversation to keep it healthy.

More to the point, marriage is a lifelong conversation that merely holds a promise of a lifetime of discovery, encouragement, discussions, and even arguments. When the dialogue within a marriage erodes, or the dynamics of the conversation do not flow freely, the relationship suffers, and our level of love and happiness within that relationship fades. It honestly comes down to the care that we take to enrich the very soil of our relationship with our partner that will help ensure a lifetime of happy, productive seasons.

Nevertheless, a successful relationship does not automatically guarantee a happy marriage. The roots of love and happiness begin with mutual respect and equality; no marriage should start without these underlying attributes. Couples can run into deep emotional issues when the obligation becomes a duty to the other or an implied right of ownership over the other.

Often we expect that once we are married, our happiness will just naturally fall into place. The reality is that we are not always going to agree, because we each see things from our own perspective. To build happiness in our marriage, we need to look at perspective, compatibility, and then fulfillment.

Perception is indeed a matter of perspective. It is like two people looking at a mountain from opposite sides. The view can be very different. Both are looking at the same mountain, but each will see a different path to the top. Take, for instance, our perspective of the mountain and our world—it changes when we climb to the top and can look down at them from the peak. When we never take a moment and look at things from another person's viewpoint or honestly listen to what he or she has to say, we will never understand why that person sees and thinks differently.

Compatibility, then, needs to start with the ability to look beyond our own point of view, or at the very least, recognize our partner's standpoint. Even if you do not always agree at first, you can negotiate a compromise that will form an acceptable foundation for living as one. We often overlook working out these negotiated agreements before marriage; we just expect to work them out during the first couple of years. However, part of our overall tolerance of each other lies within our own level of happiness, which is directly tied to our individual level of accomplishment. This means, to continue being happy after the honeymoon is over, we also need to address our needs and our desire for fulfillment.

When looking at fulfillment, we must first realize that there are two distinct types, and a deficiency in either has the capacity of tearing down any relationship. The problem is that they can come at you at the same time and often go hand in hand. We need to learn to separate the two and then distinguish the effects each has on our relationship.

The first type of fulfillment is about our earthly or physical needs. We as individuals have needs and desires, which are not just about sex but about the basics, like food, shelter, and clothing. More to the point, it is in managing our resources or the money that provides for these needs. To be even more precise, it is how we allocate what is now a shared income—our money.

The second type of fulfillment is more spiritual. These have to do with goals and achievements. We all have expectations for how we want to live our lives. These may be defined by our faith, our commitment to higher education, or our desire for a better lifestyle. Our goals might even be about the freedom to do what we love, whether it is found in a rewarding career or a creative interest. This type of fulfillment may simply encompass our need to be safe and secure in the relationship that is most important to us.

Taking into account our individual need for both types of fulfillment and the dynamics within any relationship—this is where the dialogue between partners becomes crucial, and discussions need to remain candid. These conversations need to be open-minded, impartial, and, above all, honest. Especially when we approach the more difficult problems, those mountains in our relationship, we have to stop to not only look and listen but also to see and understand our partner's perspective. This way, the two as one may find a better path up the mountain. At the very least, both need to agree to follow a shared path—the one that allows them to reach the peak, regardless of the difficulties or concessions each may need to make.

Any marriage where either partner puts his or her own self-interest ahead of the others will become harder to sustain over time. This kind of behavior can lead to misgivings, especially if it comes at a higher expense to one spouse. Building long-term happiness indeed hinges on some balanced fulfillment of individual goals. The problem is that now personal goals must be weighed against the goals of our partner and of the marriage. Again, this is where the dialogue and perspective play vital roles in our relationship. Even with compromises, we can continue to help our partner become the best he or she can be. When we do, individual goals can be met, and mutual success can be attained.

The odd thing is that the very act of encouragement and support can become more important than goals. By supporting each other as equals, the two can raise the bar within their relationship. When the bar is level, and each person has a firm footing in the relationship, a successful marriage, and a happy family can be secured. As long as the relationship continues to be mutually supportive and the conversation remains healthy, any couple can work through even the most spirited of debates. In this way, couples can weather the seasons, year in and year out, and still find happiness.

Although keeping a perspective on both types of fulfillment is essential, we also need to be mindful of other factors that can become problematic. For instance, we need to take the time to have a little fun, both as a couple and on our own. Yet even here, in our search for fun and entertainment, we are not always going to agree. Looking beyond this, we need to understand that the bickering and intolerance of all those daily annoyances are a measurement of our level of happiness.

When we start harboring a resentful attitude and tear each other down at any open opportunity, then we each need to take a step back and analyze the issues through perspective. We must let the conversation and then discovery uncover the root cause.

In many cases, it may point us back to that initial breakdown in trust. This may have been caused by an inequality with one or both types of fulfillment. More subtly, this imbalance could also have destabilized layers of openness in our daily dialogue.

In these hard times, it is even more critical to keep the dialogue balanced, respectful, and honest. At some point, regardless of the root cause, we sometimes have to walk the difficult path and take those tough steps to seek forgiveness, to truly forgive, and then move on, if we want to find healing. We may never forget what happened, but this is the starting point that will allow us to put it behind us and move forward.

When any relationship lacks mutual support and dives into deep-seated abuse, whether emotional or physical, it ceases to be a relationship. It is no longer a covenant because it violates the very nature of our relationship with God and each other. God makes few demands on us, and they can be condensed down to three truths that we must embrace: that God is the true core of your being, that your life and every person's life should be respected and is sacred and that we are all equal in the eyes of God. No sacred promise, not even the bonds of holy matrimony, can stand if it defiles these simplest of truths.

Another item to reflect on is that a healthy relationship starts with a healthy self-image. This means that we first must be comfortable and honest with ourselves before we can be with others. Periodically, when we try to resolve issues in our marriage, guidance, nurturing, and love can only take you so far. At these times, we may need to address or balance these issues from within our own selves.

If we are not careful, we can become our own worst enemy within our relationships. This really stems from the fact that we are all flawed. We are human. Sometimes the hidden beauty of a relationship is that it requires us to evaluate ourselves, and this can help us to evolve personally. Self-introspection can reveal a better path, a better course in life. Change that is forced against your will, either by nature or by others, is merely survival. Change from within, through our own intention, desire, or need, is transformational. We have all been given the tools to do this. Even though this is a personal journey of reflection, it can have a profound effect not just on you but on your relationship with your spouse and even God.

When looking at all of our relationships, the same principles of conversation apply whether this communication is with each other, God, or even nature. In our relationship with God, we spend much of our time talking the talk. We talk about our faith, its history, its customs, and its traditions. We talk about the laws, the ceremonies, the rituals, and the sacraments. We talk about God, and we pray to God. We endlessly talk. The problem is that we do not take the time to pay attention; we do not know how to listen.

Without listening, there is no conversation, and without this exchange, there is no relationship. We overlook the fact that our dialogue with God is also a two-way relationship. Built around prayer and meditation, this conversation stems from the greater peace that is at our core, the peace that is God within us. Prayer is the act of talking to God. Meditation is the act of listening to God. One leads to the other. Both, woven together, can help us uncover our peaceful core. Once revealed, peace becomes our focal point; it is our most important gift. It indeed drives our self-awareness, which expands our sense of wonder, leading to new understandings of our world and ourselves. Through this peace, we connect with God.

Enlightenment starts when we ask the questions, look for the answers, and learn something about ourselves in the process. Listening begins this process of awareness. The awareness of the deep peace within starts the dialogue with God. However, we also must accept the two mandates of the simplest of truths, which are respecting each other's life and treating each other as equals. By doing this, we can then listen with an unbiased heart. When we embrace this attitude, and our soul is at ease, the wisdom of God is revealed, and we will know in our hearts the better course to take.

When looking at the workings of our relationships, we realize that they are held together and kept healthy by the free-flowing exchanges in our daily dialogues. Considering this, one may wonder why we have so many problems. We may need to go back to the so-called beginning, to our many creation myths. The first great disservice they can imply is that there is a fundamental inequality between men and women. This alleged disparity drives a wedge in the balance and harmony that should exist between a man and a woman.

Second, they can also imply that we are born with a burden of debt, whether inherited or ancestral and as such, we are born "tainted" with an "unclean soul" or with "original sin." This is not the case; we are merely born with potential. For good or bad, this unrefined potential is defined first through our relationship with our parents. It is then further refined through the energy we exchange in all the relationships we have with others, with nature, and with God throughout our entire lifetime. These conversations are what truly define and continuously refine each of us.

Our one essential lesson in life is not whether there is any form of original sin. It has nothing to do with knowledge or our quest for greater understanding. Instead, it revolves around coping with our human needs, wants, and desires. More to the point, our essential lesson is about fulfillment. When we do not follow the two mandates of the simplest of truths—that your life and every person's life is sacred, and that we are all equal in the eyes of God—we are tempted to assert our authority, believing this will lead to greater respect and privilege. The more power we have, the further our influence takes us. In return, we expect or demand that this influence should provide us with a higher level of fulfillment at a much lower level of effort.

When we do not practice the principles of the two mandates, we allow ourselves to justify the establishment of a hierarchy—one that attempts to puts some of us second only to God. By ignoring these principles, we find ways to rationalize our dominance over those we deem lesser than ourselves. Going one step further, our creation myths also attempt to establish humankind's supremacy over our world, stating that we have a God-given right to rule over all that exists under heaven. These distractions deceive us and do not allow us to truly understand what was intended. What is important is the harmony in our relationships, that personal connection with God, with the rest of humanity, and with our planet.

Our obsession with ever-greater levels of self-fulfillment entices us to try to be like God in the way we perceive God to be. We strive for authority, power, privilege, and respect, but we will ultimately be corrupted and destroyed by our quest for these things. The promise of power is the effortless fulfillment of needs and desires, but one person's ease and comfort are often gained by someone else's burden, expense, or outright exploitation. It then becomes disparity, which sows discontent and hate. This opens the floodgates of other temptations and sins. Our creation myths can be deceptively immoral because they can propagate and sustain our true sin—humankind's arrogant and self-serving pursuit of entitlement.

For most people, good and evil go hand in hand, so we often believe in God as well as a great deceiver. Actually, our own actions, good or bad, have always been in our own hands. Still, we want to blame a great evil rather than ourselves for our own bad choices. Pure evil is rejecting God, our inner peace, and the two mandates of the three simple truths and replacing them with our selfish desires. Our attempt to establish a supreme authority over others or the earth's resources for personal gain has always been one of our greatest faults.

Even today, there are blatant deceptions in the myths that we propagate as part of our faith or our belief systems. The most prevailing is still interpreted as a proclamation that a man has been given dominion over his wife or at the very minimum, the husband is the head of the marriage and family. Another is that we are the preeminent masters of our world. Regarding our environment, our natural assumption is that we are free to use its resources solely and uncompromisingly for our own benefit and profit. We can blind ourselves to the fact that this is also a relationship and can quickly become exploitive, abusive, destructive, and ultimately unsustainable, which invariably leads to an imbalance in nature.

Once in motion, unbalanced or lopsided relationships tend to develop control issues. When we rob nature of its vitality, stripping the earth's flora and fauna to near extinction, or poison it with our waste the further out of our control things become, and the closer we move to our own destruction. We overlook the fact that our connection with nature is also a relationship, which follows the same rules as our personal relationships. Our dilemma becomes how to balance our needs with what our environment can support, without comprising its long-term integrity. Again, this is where perspective and an ongoing dialogue play critical roles.

To keep the earth healthy, there needs to be an unbiased conversation with each other regarding our planet and a balanced, free-flowing exchange of energy between our environment and ourselves. To do this, we need to stop, look, listen and then analyze the information we get back from our environment. We need to take a sustainable approach to what we acquire from nature and then take the same measured attitude to what and how we give back to our planet. When it comes to our environment, we must look past our own point of view. We must recognize that exploitation, of each other or of nature, is equally degrading in the end. When it comes to our environment, no matter the scale, its misuse can potentially be as destructive to us as it is to nature.

Humanity has inherited the guardianship of the ultimate gift, this planet we call home. As such, we are all responsible for managing our world wisely. We need to learn how to have a dialog with the environment and then learn to live in harmony with our surroundings if we want to continue to exist on this planet. Again, it honestly comes down to the care that we take to enrich the very soil of our relationship with our world that will help ensure generations of healthy and productive seasons.

The conversation encompasses our relationships with each other, with God, and with nature. It is the negotiated exchange, the spirited debate, and the harmony of our dialogue. It is about listening, analyzing, and discovering. It is about learning, about sharing, and about love. The conversation is about the relationships, the connections, the meeting points, and the cycles of interchanging energy between the two. It is about our earthly, human, and spiritual ecology.

Walking out of the Dark: Part Four

Winter's Renewing Spirit

Faded and meager, the warmth of the setting sun as it sinks lower on the yellow-orange horizon, the cooling days of change set the stage for a transition, an ageless lesson in perseverance.

Dreary and withered, the bleakness of winter sets in and slowly reinvents the landscape, as the days grow shorter and more sullen, a deep cold creeps into the frost-touched terrain of the mind.

Lonely and dejected, the earth yawns and gone are the colors of brighter days, all things worn-down and shaded in greys, the landscape shivers, and recoils as it collapses into listlessness.

Exhausted and disheveled, the land drifts into an uneasy but deep meditation, a world lost between the thoughts, here the weedy underbrush of fear, anger, and hate succumb to winter's cold clarity.

Faint and unfriendly, the night sighs as unrelenting snow begins to drop, the darkened sky turns ashen as the falling of the giant flakes intensifies, yet felt within the snowfall is a feeling of peace and serenity.

Desolate and muffled, locked in the grip of introspection all echoes die as snow obscures everything, the fierce blizzard begins to howl, frosty is the breath that rattles the naked trees and stills the restless water of thought.

Timeless and serene, a cold comfort is wrapped in the fresh blanket of insulating snow, thick is the tranquility that protects *the mind's soil from the icy winds, a weight that rebalances our intertwined emotions.*

Peace and patience, there is an awareness in the quietness, for some things must freeze and wither to clear the ground, for unseen are the many gifts that await an opportunity for us to discover and cultivate.

Intentions and aspirations, fresh thoughts hidden in the promise of the roots and seeds, hope rises as enlightenment pushes up toward consciousness, spring envisioning and nurturing our long-term integrity.

Spirit and evolution, the sap surges just below the surface bringing with it an energy, the ever-growing streams of wisdom expand our perspective, an insight only revealed by living through all the seasons.

Awakened and renewed, the days quicken to thaw the frost-entrenched earth of the mind, buds leaf out to capture the warmth of the gleaming sunlight, gradually unveiled are the blooming possibilities of the soul.

Realization and transformation, the winter's inner-peace enriches and renews the spirit, clearing the land and leading the mind into a different state, an enigmatic character that ushers in a newfound era of growth and wellbeing.

Arthur made one sweep through the inn and even checked the roof just in case Mairwyn was there, but she was nowhere to be found. He eventually ended up at the front desk to talk to Olena. She insisted on fixing a lunch, so he stayed and spent some time visiting and catching up with her on what was going on in the inn and in town. By the end of lunch, she too was not sure where her daughter had gone. "Perhaps she has gone off to the market," she said as he left.

From there, Arthur set off for the brickworks. To his surprise, he still knew most of the people who worked there. Even so, he did not recognize any of the others as the old man he knew as Philthy.

"Hello," said a raspy voice from somewhere behind him. He turned around. "Might you be Arthur?" asked the man.

"Yes," Arthur replied. The older man in front of him had tightly trimmed hair, was clean-shaven, a bit round at the waist, and slightly taller than Arthur.

"I thought it was you, and that you may have been looking for me. I am Mathias, but you may have only known me as Philthy."

"You are right about that, I would never have recognized you as the man I met what seems like so long ago," said Arthur.

"Your aunt kept telling me that you would show up when the time was right. She is a very wise woman. Do you have time to walk with me? I...I need to talk with you...for a little while."

"You saved my life, Mathias; the least I can do is walk with you and listen to what you have to say."

Mathias motioned for Arthur to follow. Both men turned and headed out of the Brickyard in the general direction of the inn.

"That day...that day when we parted, when you told me who you were and where you were from, and you asked me to find your aunt at her inn," Mathias began. Arthur nodded, and Mathias stopped and turned to face him. "The truth is that...that I knew this place because I was born here. I knew your aunt and uncle, I knew your mum, and...and I knew your dad."

"You knew my dad!" a surprised Arthur exclaimed.

"We were childhood friends before the earthquake destroyed most of the town," replied Mathias.

They walked on in silence even though Arthur's thoughts turned over a half a dozen questions he wanted to ask Mathias about his dad. Mathias seemed to be in no hurry. He set a plodding pace, which appeared to Arthur as having nothing to do with a disability or his age.

"Truth be told," Mathias continued after they had walked about a block, "I was deathly afraid of coming back here, but I promised you that I would deliver your message. Anyway, I had other reasons why I could not let you down. I also promised you that I would stay sober, and I did. That started one change in my life for the better. Mind you, at the time I started traveling to this village, I did not care about how far I needed to travel. Yet every step toward this place was one step closer to the one thing I'd been running from all my life."

Mathias stopped again. They were on the main road through town, which was the longer route back to the inn from the Brickyard. Mathias's eyes seemed to be fixed on something down the street. Arthur looked in the direction he was staring but saw nothing out of the ordinary.

Mathias moved on. "When I finally arrived, I cleaned myself up the best I could and then set off to find your aunt at the inn. I inquired about Kaisa at the front desk, and when she said 'Speaking,' I couldn't find my voice." Mathias stopped again and turned to Arthur. "Then she did the most amazing thing. She smiled and said, 'Mathias, you old coot,' and she came round the desk and gave me a hug." By now, Mathias had tears streaming down his cheeks. They continued to stroll on, but Mathias was quiet for a while.

"You know," he said, "she was the first person to call me by my real name in over twenty years. I don't know how she knew, but she did, and she welcomed me like an old friend as if nothing bad had ever happened. We have had many long conversations since then, and again, I can thank you for that."

"So, what did happen?" asked Arthur. By now, they had stopped in the courtyard on the east side of the inn and were standing near a very old-looking statue that was a new addition to the property.

Mathias sat down on one of the stone benches. "Do you know who this statue represents?" Arthur shook his head, and Mathias went on. "It's the founder of the town. Before the earthquake, it stood in the town square. It's also supposed to be a likeness of one of your ancestors. I found it a while back. It was half buried in a pile of rubble, so I dug it out. Your aunt was excited about the find and had it brought here."

"You know the story about the earthquake?" asked Mathias. Arthur nodded his head. "You know the stories about what the town was like back then?" Again, he nodded. "Do you know how your grandfather died?"

"He died in the earthquake with so many others," said Arthur.

"No, Arthur," he said. Mathias was shaking, and tears were again welling up in his eyes. "My father killed him—with this." He reached into his pocket and pulled out a hunk of brick about the size of his palm.

Burning anger started to flare up inside Arthur. He felt its heat in his cheeks, and he turned to leave.

"Please, Arthur, please let me finish." Arthur stopped but did not turn around. "I was just a boy when it happened. Your grandfather and his family were being forced to leave town. I didn't understand why. My mum only told me that they had broken the rules, and back then, the town had some crazy rules. Us kids at that time thought it made the adults act weird."

"Your dad was my best friend. We used to play together at the park—the park that is now the cemetery just up the road. I did not know why his family had to be paraded out of town. I didn't know why we had to go watch the procession. I didn't want to see my friend forced to leave town, and I really didn't want him to see me standing in the crowd, so I tried to stay hidden behind my mum."

"For the longest time, I just stood there, looking down. For whatever reason, I started kicking at a loose brick in the curb. Then it happened—it broke free. I heard Mum gasp, and my father let out a long string of profanities. I remember that he slapped me so hard I fell into the gutter. Then suddenly, he picked up the broken piece of brick and threw it at your grandfather, who was just then passing by."

By now, Arthur had sat down next to Mathias and put an arm around his shoulders. The old man was a mess of emotions.

"The memory of those long moments that followed haunts me still. You know, your aunt told me that your dad never held a grudge against me and said I shouldn't have anything to be sorry about, but I have never been able to forgive my father or myself. I am very sorry for what happened to your family that day, Arthur."

"I think my aunt is right about one thing, and I think you really have nothing to be sorry about," Arthur replied. "And if she says my father didn't hold it against you, neither will I. But I do think the repercussions of that one moment of anger have caused enough damage in your life. I cannot give you my grandfather's forgiveness or my father's, but if it helps, I can give you mine. I forgive you Mathias and thank you for sharing this with me, but now I think I need to talk with my aunt."

After a pause, Arthur asked, "Are you going to be all right?" Mathias nodded. "You will always have my friendship, Mathias."

"Thank you, Arthur," replied Mathias.

Back at the inn, Arthur stopped by his aunt's bedroom, and they talked for a short while about Mathias and his own family history. He was not allowed to stay long because of his aunt who shooed him away again, to go find Mairwyn.

When Arthur arrived on the roof, there was no one there. The inn's roof was reasonably flat but sloped gradually from the front to the back. It was surrounded on three sides by a chest-high wall. Across the entire width of the front side of the inn, a second wooden roof protected the rooftop. Long after the earthquake, his father and uncle had added the rooftop garden; this was done in celebration of finishing many years of repairs to the old inn.

They had intended it to be used for parties and weddings, but to Arthur's knowledge, it had never been used. Arthur found a spot along the front wall where he could see the front courtyard and watch the sunset.

"Now, isn't this a surprise," said a voice in a very flat tone. "I had not heard you were back."

Arthur turned; he had been lost in thought and did not hear her approach. Arthur stared at the woman walking toward him. "Hello, Wyn," he said. She stopped a short distance from him and leaned against the wall, her arms crossed over her chest.

"I guess you are here to bury your aunt and sell off your inheritance," she said in the same flat tone.

"That's not a fair thing to say," Arthur replied.

"I suppose not. So why are you here, Artie?" She used a nickname that she knew he hated. "Did my mom send for you, or did your aunt finally decide to send a message? God knows she wouldn't let me tell you about her illness."

"I am here because..." he said and then stopped. "Because I needed to be home. In fact, the rest of my stuff should be here in a couple of days. Only now, I find out my aunt is dying." Arthur paused again and swallowed hard. "And you, you are leaving too. Home is starting to look as empty and gloomy as my apartment in the city."

"Who told you that I'm leaving? Was it my mom? I know it wasn't your aunt, because nobody was supposed to tell her."

"Well, I don't know how she knew your plans, but she did, and she was the one who told me. Aunt Kaisa and I had a long talk this morning, and she told me about her cancer. At the end of our conversation, she made me promise to go talk with two people—Mathias and *you*. She did not tell me about what or why, and honestly, nothing she could have said could have prepared me for what Mathias told me this afternoon," he paused. "I'm guessing that she wants me to try to persuade you to stay, but based on your attitude, I don't really think there is anything I can say to change your mind...about leaving." He paused again. "But if you can spare a few more minutes, there is something else I want...I need to talk to you about." Arthur hesitated.

"Fine, I'll give you a few minutes," Mairwyn replied.

"I wanted to tell you...I wanted to say...I'm sorry. I'm sorry for not being the friend I should have been over the last couple of years, for not writing more often, for writing the letters I did when I did write, and for pushing our friendship aside."

"Why are you telling me this now, Arthur? *Why*?" Her voice broke, and Arthur could see her eyes welling up, tears threatening to roll down her cheeks.

"When I was in my first year at the university, it was the letters from home that helped me get through some very tough times. By the end of that first year, I looked forward to your letters. Your letters always seemed to show up when I needed to be cheered up, and your letters meant the most to me." Mairwyn said nothing, so he continued.

"I only ever had a few casual friends in the city. By the end of that third year at the university, through those letters, *you* were the best friend that I had. It was you whom I felt I could freely talk to or, I guess, write to and tell about the things going on in my life. It was you whom I was most comfortable with in sharing my thoughts and feelings." Arthur turned and looked towards the setting sun; the sun was very low on the horizon and sky was full of color, the ribbons of clouds that streaked across the sky were mostly pinks and oranges.

"Then that bloody revolution happened, and I was swept up into some terrible things. It changed me, Wyn, and I haven't really been myself or felt like my old self since."

Arthur had not been looking at Mairwyn. When he did, she had one hand over her mouth and tears streaming down her face. "I knew at some point that you had deeper feelings for me, Wyn, and at first I tried to ignore it. Looking back, it was a time in my life that I could have used a trusted friend like you, but I pushed you away, and I'm sorry, Wyn. I'm sorry for hurting you."

There was a long pause before Arthur could find his voice again. Mairwyn had turned away, but she had not left or said anything. "I know I can't persuade you to stay, but would you consider staying at least until after Aunt Kaisa passes?" After what seemed to be a long pause, he softly added, "Please, Wyn; I don't think I can do this alone."

Mairwyn spun around. "No, Arthur!" she yelled. "If you want me to stay, you need to—you have to—promise me that you won't leave again and that you won't sell the inn or leave *me* again."

Arthur reached out and wrapped his arms around her, hugged her tightly, and whispered in her ear, "I promise, Wyn, I promise. I'm home to stay."

For Arthur, the embrace was surreal; this woman was not the same gawky girl he once knew, this Mairwyn, with her odd but wholesome beauty, was someone he barely recognized. Yet in her presence, in the weight of her arms around him, in the warmth of her body, he felt something, something so comfortable and familiar he did not want to let go, but the moment did not last.

"Arthur," she whispered and then reluctantly pushed away from him, her eyes cast downward, "I knew you were here this morning, but I purposely avoided you. After I learned of your arrival, I had actually decided to leave early without speaking to you, but at the last minute, I decided that…that I needed to say good-bye. Then I couldn't find you anywhere. I asked my mom, but she was no help. She didn't know where you had gone. Your aunt was no help either. I was angry when I came up here; I always come up here when I'm mad, or sad, or lonely." She stepped around him, walked over to the wall, and turned to gaze into what was left of the sunset. "I was genuinely surprised to see you up here, but I was so damn mad at you, Arthur."

"I don't blame you, Wyn, for being angry with me."

"You don't understand, Arthur; I have loved you since we were kids. I loved you because you had a way of making me smile. You listened to me and tried to make me feel better when I was upset. You were there for me, especially on those days when I had been endlessly teased at school. You made me feel that I mattered and that I was somebody."

"I loved you because you cared about people. You, who had lost so much in your life—first your dad and then your mum—you would go out of your way to help others. I loved you because you were a good person, Arthur. I always thought that you were the one I would spend my life with." She paused.

"Right after you left for college, I was furious at your aunt because she was the one who sent you away. At some point, she had to sit me down for a bit of a chat and clear the air. She told me the story of why it was important for you to leave. She also suggested that I write letters to you, but when I did, I should write them from my heart. I did that, Arthur. I did that." She paused again and then went on.

"I used to come up here and watch the sun go down and imagine us getting married in this rooftop garden or just watch the road, hoping to see you coming home. I thought someday you might come over that low hill just behind the old town wall, but you never did."

"There came the point when I knew that I had lost you, and I was heartbroken. I was sad and angry and felt foolish at the same time. Yet I would still come up here to watch the sunset. Sometimes I'd wake up early and wander up here to watch the sun rise over the mountains. I found a sense of peace here, and it gave me the strength to go on, to move on with my life."

"Now I'm torn again, I want to stay Arthur, but I don't know if my heart can take it, because...because I'm still in love with you. I just don't know, Arthur...I don't know if I'm what you are truly looking for, and I'm not sure if I can trust you or my own heart again."

"Then don't, Wyn," Arthur said. "Don't give your love to the Arthur of yesterday. Let me, the Arthur that stands in front of you now, earn it back if I truly can. Just give me a chance to get to know the Mairwyn that stands before me now, the Mairwyn of today."

Mairwyn said nothing and then she turned away from Arthur. She leaned against the chest-high wall again, putting both arms on top of it. For a moment, Arthur just watched Mairwyn gaze into the sunset and then stepped forward and joined her there. They both watched in silence as the sun finished sinking into the horizon. Just before the sun disappeared, Arthur felt Mairwyn slip her arm around his and leaned her head against his shoulder.

From out of the shadows two fugitive figures crept towards the stairs. Once they reached the safety of the steps, Kaisa and Olean scrambled down the stairway like two giddy school girls and ducked back into the inn.

* * *

In early autumn, Arthur, Mairwyn, Olena, and Mathias buried Kaisa next to her beloved Zachary. The following summer, Arthur and Mairwyn were married in the inn's newly remodeled rooftop garden.

SECTION 5

Moving Forward

When asked if life is a matter of faith or science, I would tell you that I honestly do not care how or why we came into being. It is neither important nor relevant. We are here, and that is all that needs to be said. Yet, we spend our days arguing and fighting over thousands of different points and all the conceivable details. In the end, those sentiments are inconsequential. What does matter is how we live our lives today, in our moment in history. More importantly, what matters is our ability to treat each other with respect and honesty. That we each live our own life with integrity and wisdom and do not turn away from compassion or harden our hearts against forgiveness.

Our Legacy

When we think of our legacy, we tend to think on a grand scale, entirely in the context of our own self-worth. For most, it is about striving to obtain goals. To some, it is about seeing and experiencing as much of the world as possible. For others, it may be about putting their own unique stamp on their job or field of work. Still, others may attempt to make a difference in their country or the world. All of these may contribute in part to one kind of legacy, but in actuality, our only true legacy is our children.

Yet, there is more to our true legacy than just giving birth or fathering a child. While these roles are within the very fabric of our earthly state of being, there is more to it than being a genetic donor to the next generation. The unseen element that influences our lives is our spiritual nature. That effect gives our parenting a deeper meaning and purpose. When fully embraced, it is this higher goal that really defines our legacy. It becomes a dominant driving force behind the one simple promise that defines tomorrow, and that is ensuring life's continuation.

Each of us is the legacy of our grandparents, not our parents. For our parents, we are a promise toward that end. Only when we fulfill our part of that promise by having our own children will our parents' legacy be fulfilled. It then falls on us to raise our children, the next generation, with the hope that they will, in turn, fulfill this basic promise. We endeavor to do this not only because it is a part of life and our family's future but also for the greater legacy of all of humanity.

We are creatures of nature, and as such, we are embedded in the circles of life. In this, we are no different from any other creature on this planet. Our prime objective is self-preservation, and our prime directive is procreation. Our bodies are hard-wired with the will to survive and a desire to reproduce, which exacts a considerable amount of control over us physically and emotionally. These are the two primary factors within our earthly nature, and it, directly and indirectly, influences our lives and our relationships with each other. It also spills over into our relationships with God and ultimately with our environment. Despite being chained to the fear and anger that comes from living in an often cruel and unforgiving world, we have been given the tools to cope with these earthly natures and be successful.

We as human beings have been drawn up from out of this rich pool of life that exists on this planet, and we have been made self-aware. Our first spiritual gift may have started in part with our curiosity, our sense of wonder about the world around us. This led us to new discoveries and new insights, giving us a greater understanding of our surroundings. Our awareness of ourselves in relationship to our environment is what allowed us to change a learned behavior, to adapt, and to survive. From this reasoning frame of mind, we have been able to adjust to new or shifting environments and prepare for the changing of the seasons. This willingness to adapt is found in our own will to survive, but it also wells up from our deep-seated desire for our children to survive. This, in part, has forced us to look beyond the present and think about tomorrow.

The gifts of the spirit have provided us with our ever-inquisitive and continuously reaching mind. They have been infused by God into our earthly characteristics. These same gifts allow us to assign a positive or negative value to everything and everyone we interact with, in our world. For good or for ill, these spiritual gifts give us the ability to love but also to hate. The effects of these intertwined natures not only allow us to transcend our environment but they can enhance our most personal relationships and improve our broader connections with the rest of humanity.

Within each of us, where the two natures converge, is that peaceful spot that bridges the gap between our individual self and God. We have described God in many different ways, but the easiest way to recognize the presence of God is by the feeling of peace.

Regardless of where you are in the world or the circumstances when you sense peace, it blooms from the deepest depth of your being. When we actively seek the peace at our core, it is both calming and invigorating. When combined with prayer and meditation, seeking and embracing that peace can indeed become transformational.

That being said, we are not being called to be like God in any way, shape, or form. We are drawn into a greater fulfillment by the gifts of enlightenment so we can become better people. Yet these gifts are not given lightly. We are also called to take a more responsible attitude. Our prime spiritual objective is to allow peace and God to be revealed within us. Our prime spiritual directives are to strive to treat each other as equals and to remember to regard each other's lives as sacred. We must remain grounded in our humanity to live our lives by these simplest of truths.

Regardless of whether we are born male or female, we are equipped with the same enlightened human brain. We may not see things from the same perspective, but we possess the same powerful and advanced thinking mind. The key is not just unlocking the potential that we are born with but also nurturing and growing the potential our children are born with. In our role as parents, our earthly nature imparts the basic tendency or the compulsion to raise our children to independence and adulthood. However, our spiritual enlightenment takes us far beyond what this tendency can offer. It introduces us to the deep bonds of love, the strength of which can dramatically increase our level of success over our older, more animalistic nature.

Love is our deepest expression of nurturing and guidance. It is our decision or our commitment to take care of someone or something despite the hardships and sacrifices. Some would also define our most profound love as unconditional, which is often reserved for the love a parent has for their children. We also tend to apply the same label to God's love for us. But we can never hope to understand or comprehend the true scope of God's love or unconditional love. Unconditional love for us is still the same decision to love, but it is a commitment that needs to be made every day, regardless of what occurred yesterday.

It could be said that from the very earliest roots of humanity, our ability to love expanded because we placed a higher value on our children and their well-being. This, in part, is driving our spiritual and social evolution. Love is the currency of the spirit, the currency of God. These dynamics are part of what is at the true heart of our humanity, and it gives purpose to our lives. It is love that builds trust in our relationships. Love provides those two essential tools for parenthood: nurturing and guidance. These tools help us pass along our knowledge and elevate our level of success in life. They help define and refine what our quintessential role in life is.

The role of a parent will always be the most significant job of our lifetime. Yet parenthood is also one of the most demanding burdens we will ever assume because it takes an extraordinary amount of time and energy to be successful. Like any other task in our world, success is never guaranteed. With parenthood, it is indeed a job that is never really done, because it is a lifelong relationship. It is our chief responsibility, our supreme challenge; our greatest and most rewarding task. It is the ultimate investment because it holds the promise of a tomorrow because we continue to pass along the gift of life and the gift of love.

There is no greater joy in life than holding your newborn child. There is no deeper satisfaction than seeing your children growing and doing well for themselves. There is no stronger sense of fulfillment than a hug from your grandchild. Yet we also understand that there will always be things that are out of our control. With parenthood comes an enormous emotional risk, perils that can break our hearts and shred the soul. There is no greater sorrow than seeing your child suffering or losing a child, and no greater sense of loss than losing your mother or father. There is no more overwhelming feeling of helplessness as profound than being left behind, left alone, pushed aside, unwanted, or abandoned.

Yet within those gifts of the spirit come the compassion and the strength to reach out to those in their time of need and lift them up. Regardless of our own burdens, we have the ability to give them hope, to help them move forward and to carry on.

This too is a natural extension of parenthood, a measure of that central role in life, and an echo of the currency of God flowing through us all.

The Promise

It could be said that the children of the last half dozen decades have been raised to reach for life's golden ring. Many in the world's highly industrialized nations have come to view success as the ability to become exactly who and what they want to be in life. We measure our achievements by meeting or surpassing our educational goals. We then move forward to find that perfect career. We spend years building our success so we can fill our own self-absorbed world with our every need and desire. We are always seeking to achieve that next big goal, the one that can take us to the next level and beyond.

Our individual identity is often solely based on self. We forget that our parents worked hard to provide us with the best opportunities so we could succeed in life. Quite likely, many parents are more than happy in their children's accomplishments. But what is the point of our individual success if there is no one following in our footsteps? Throughout our lifetime, we make impressions in the sands of life. But if there is no one walking behind us, following our example, what happens when our footprints stop? That path paced out by us, our parents, and our grandparents will end. Life will continue to ebb and flow, but those unique imprints we have made in life will be forgotten and lost with time.

We can father a child; we can give birth to a baby. When we do, we give life to the next generation, and in doing so, we give humanity a tomorrow. At birth, we are the purest expression of life's purpose. We then quickly grow deep roots in the circles of life. Unfortunately, we can also become lost within them. When we explore the different directions life can take us, this journey can lead us to places where we can lose sight of our most essential role. When this role is unfulfilled, whether it is by choice or not, a thread of humanity is broken, and in the end, that unique thread is likely lost forever.

Within our social circles, individual choices push us to reject the idea of a broken thread because individualism eclipses the importance of that essential role. Yet, this should not be considered an unrecoverable situation. Instead, it is understandable and even acceptable. Other threads of humanity will step up and replace those broken and missing threads, and life continues.

What we may not be able to recover from is when an idea gains enough support that our society turns away from that essential role and replaces it with a distorted and egocentric viewpoint that gives no thought to tomorrow or to humanity's long-term sustainability. The more we, as a society, move away from life's natural course, the more vulnerable our future becomes. If we do not stay true to our biology, in time, our social ideologies may tip the scales against the future, and this will put large parts of humanity at risk. In the long term, society's greatest losses may come when today's most talented, creative, intellectual, and gifted minds pass away without making an impression on the gene pool of tomorrow.

So many people today have lost sight of tomorrow. They cannot see, or they do not care, that there is more to tomorrow than the next goal. There is more to fulfillment than our own wants and goals. When we live in a world of me, we forget that true happiness does not come from filling our lives with things or going to new and exotic places. True happiness is built in the relationships we form, grow, and nurture with others throughout our journey in life. Long-term happiness is found in the relationships that are important to us, like friends, family, our spouse, and God. It should also be said that an even broader, more transformational sense of fulfillment and happiness blossoms in the bonds we form with our children. It is revealed slowly through the time we spend raising our children into adulthood. As parents mold their children's lives, parents themselves are ultimately transformed by this relationship.

When a parent is fully involved, the emphasis shifts away from self, and this is not a smooth transition. More often than not, we begin to resent parenthood as a loss of independence or a loss of our person. Yet parenthood becomes one of the most essential journeys we will ever embark on because we have to let go of some of our selfishness. For both mothers and fathers, the experience of parenthood brings to light, a new depth of meaning in their lives. It fundamentally changes the way they view life and redefines what is truly important.

Marriage and family require a measure of self-sacrifice, but this keeps us anchored in life. It keeps us engaged in the relationships that are the most important to us. Yet it is parenthood, our relationship with our children that defines our true success. That said, parenthood should not be considered a career, because it is not. It is part of the very fabric of life. It is a natural part of living. In addition, parenthood should not be contingent on your job or your career path. At every level of employment within any society, the career should be made to accommodate parenthood because it is that important.

The hidden cost of delaying marriage or waiting to start a family can be staggeringly high. Fertility is never guaranteed and waiting only tilts the balance against you. For some people, not being able to have children may feel like a life path that is slowly becoming obscured by the wind-blown sands of time. Certainly, this could end up being their legacy if they chose to do nothing with their talents, by which they could have made a positive difference in the life of even one child. The same applies to those who choose not to have children, or who remain single. The parental role applies to everyone, whether those children are your own or not. This social, parental aspect is essential as it helps assure the future success of our children and our humanity.

Through every generation, parents have always had expectations of their children, though those expectations have evolved both culturally and spiritually. The first responsibility of any parent is teaching his or her children to safely navigate a world that can often be cruel and unforgiving. By example, parents need to show their children how to cope with the stress that can develop from everyday situations within their surroundings. Next, parents need to teach their children the simplest of truths. Parents should show them how to find and draw their strength from the deep peace within, from God within. They then need to guide by example, how to treat others fairly and with respect.

Only after this groundwork has been established can parents start to build a successful adult. The goal is or should be to deliver a conscientious, well-adjusted, self-sufficient, self-motivated, and sexually responsible adult. To do this, parents should try to provide their children with the best opportunities they can and an education that will help ensure their success. Children, in turn, must come to understand that those opportunities are not given lightly and that they also need to take on a responsible attitude to make the most of the opportunities their parents and others have provided for them.

As children grow into adulthood, their parents need to continue to clarify that life is about the relationships that surround them. Our children must recognize that we are all interconnected, not just with our family but with the rest of humanity, to God, and even nature. Our children need to eventually realize that the greatest gifts in life are found not just in their friends and family but also in their own journey down the path of parenthood.

Children are our greatest asset, and every child should be allowed to grow to his or her fullest potential. It is this that will help guarantee their happiness and future success, and it starts with a quality education, which falls back to the parents. Instruction in all matters of life is the best gifts parents can give their children. Simply put, education has always been important, and it is even more essential in our modern world. But that responsibility does not stop with the parents. At every level of humanity, access to education is the finest gift society can provide to every child because those educated minds will become society's greatest assets.

Tomorrow's success truly relies on the groundwork we provide, and this lives in the promise of our children. Regardless of our level of success, however, those who follow us should always keep an eye on the horizon. Our adult children should never underestimate the importance of giving of themselves, to deliver and provide a tomorrow for that generation just beyond them.

We were not merely gifted with our time in this world or our circumstances in life. Those who came before us paid for this. Their success simply meant that they did not turn their eyes away from what was truly important. Yet our parents' success does not ensure ours, just as their failures do not guarantee that we will fail. So, too, our own achievements cannot ensure the success of our children or the generation that follows them if they and we do not stay focused and keep looking forward.

The promise is what puts the future in the present and keeps it in our hearts, but it cannot exist merely in the singular and solely within. For each of us, everything started within the family, and it is continued through the family. However, this runs deeper than just our family, our children, or even our grandchildren. In a broader sense, it is bigger in scope than the roots of parenting, which are nurturing and guidance. It also encourages the wider relationship we have with the rest of humanity through respect, honesty, integrity, and wisdom. These are the other defining principles. They are the living soil that rests upon the bedrock of the simplest of truths.

The promise lives in those who have been delivered into our care, for they have not been given lightly. Every child is born with potential, each holds a promise of tomorrow. The promise is honoring the legacy of our grandparents by fulfilling the legacy of our parents. It is about taking on the responsibility to nurture and guide, to pass along the principles of respect and honesty, which hopefully will encourage our children to develop a sense of integrity and wisdom. These contributions should not only be a part of our personal family legacy, but they must also be expanded, so it includes that broader legacy of humanity which is fulfilled through all of our children. The promise is indeed the gift of new life, yet our most meaningful legacy is the love we have given our children, and they have passed on to all of their children.

Love is the greatest gift that we will ever receive from our parents—the same love that was passed along to them by their parents and grandparents. Our legacy is also a legacy of love that, when fed by the gifts of the spirit, is rooted in the principles found in the living soil and is supported by the bedrock of the simplest of truths, challenges us to be better people. Love's legacy indeed has the power to transcend the generations, but it can also be like a great tree that looks solid and strong but can swiftly be cut down or suddenly be blown over. Yet despite this, love has an even higher power to quietly spring forth and begin again, renewed. Love is the one thing that does not die when we do because we gave it to our family, our children, and our friends, and it lives on in them.

Some might think that hate is similar to love in that it can be passed down to the next generation. Unlike love, however, hate cannot renew itself. It is forced onto others by those who ignore or reject the simplest of truths. Once kindled, hate can smolder in our hearts for a lifetime and can quickly flare up and spread on wild, angry winds. Only peace can extinguish the fires of hatred, quiet the winds of anger, and calm the tides of fear. This can only happen when we first recognize the importance of the peace within, the God within, and embrace it.

Building Tomorrow

Our children are our future and tomorrow belongs to them, but the responsibility for their future success starts with us. Today, there is a lot of pressure on parents regarding how well they raise and mentor their children. But, there is so much more to be considered nowadays. We need to pay attention to all the details that could affect our children through the endless interactions of our high-tech society and ever-changing world. This means that every one of us needs to be proactively looking at all the new and different factors that could negatively affect our primary task in life, parenthood. We should always be watching, even for the small, seemingly insignificant things and be mindful of how they could influence tomorrow.

We need to look at all the issues. Not just in terms of their effect on raising a child but the long term effects on them in becoming a well-balanced adult. It is also in how we define our own views about life and how our society views success and wealth. We also need to look at the issues regarding self—how our obsession with self can ultimately affect our future or negate it. Unfortunately, society in general and even parents often overlook or underestimate some of the more critical matters, such as adequately teaching children how to build healthy relationships outside or inside their family or sufficiently preparing our teenage children for their adult sexual lives.

On this last one, we all need to understand that sex is our body's prime directive. It is a bodily function, and as such has its own set processes to ensure its successful completion. That means that no matter the status of our relationship with our partner, once the process of arousal is set in motion, our bodies will work relentlessly toward the fulfillment of that mission.

This is essentially true in different ways for both men and women. However, it is not equally taught to our boys and girls. Sex is one of our most potent earthly natures, but again, thanks to our spiritual gifts, we can learn to live in harmony with these earthly forces, and this harmony revolves around the relationship between the two. Only a healthy relationship can temper desire and provide the type of fulfillment that fuels true long-term happiness.

Throughout the ages, the art of developing healthy relationships has been an often overlooked or undervalued aspect of parenting. This shortsightedness is exacerbated when women are not viewed as equal to men or when society in general views them as noncitizens with few or no rights or privileges. The message we must instill in all of our children is that we are all equal, regardless of our sex or the color of our skin.

For teenagers, they need to understand that even though their bodies may be physically capable of sex, emotionally, they are quite likely completely unprepared. This is even more essential now in our high-tech age. It is essential for our daughters, so they have the time to develop confidence in themselves and their relationship skills and to ensure that they are not exploited emotionally or physically. This may be even more critical for our sons, so they have time to develop the skills to form and maintain healthy relationships with girls—relationships not based solely on a self-fulfilling urge for sex or the exploitive desire for sex without caring about the consequences.

As teenagers transition into their adult sexuality, parents need to help them understand that it is more than just a physical act. With sex comes a greater responsibility to themselves and their partners. Building the relationship balances and tempers the physical. The reason we humans are different from other animals is that wrapped around our physical being is our spiritual nature, and this is what allows relationships to grow and bonds to form with others. A teenager simply has a lot of growing to do, both emotionally and spiritually. Maturity can only be achieved with time, through the wisdom they gain from their interactions, experiences, and relationships. Learning how to have a healthy relationship is difficult enough without the added pressure of sex and the life-changing consequence of parenthood.

Today more than ever, parents should instill in their teenage children the integrity and wisdom to make better choices for themselves before they find themselves at that point of no return, running blindly into a potentially hazardous intersection.

On the one hand, we provide contraceptives to our teens to prevent disease and unwanted pregnancy, but the possible side effect or the hidden risk is that it could still negatively affect their health and their path in life. More importantly, sex without maturity, respect, and a solid understanding of relationships can adversely affect their self-worth and the way they view and how they define themselves later in life.

On the other hand, we stifle sexuality in the worst possible ways. We often define it in many negative and even threatening ways, but not for what it truly is—a healthy and natural function of the body. The potential side effect or the hidden risk here is that it actually could be harmful to our children's adult psyche, damage their sexual attitudes, and undermine their overall happiness later in life. It can even impair and complicate their ability to form and maintain a healthy sexual relationship with their spouse.

Within our modern society, we do not always take on the responsibility to encourage our children in, or even show them by example, the art of building healthy relationships. This is especially true if we do not take the time to be the kind of parents who engage and encourage our children to be the best they can be today so they can carry those lessons forward into tomorrow.

All that said, another factor that plays a huge role in propagating change in our present lifestyle is birth control. Granted, not many would dispute the benefits that contraceptives have given our contemporary society. Yet this marvel of modern science is promoting some less-than-positive side effects, and it is directly influencing our precepts of sex, marriage, and family.

In some respects, we have always seen children as an inevitable and often-overwhelming burden that interferes with our independence and our path to success. Now, couple this viewpoint with our control over conception. Having a child is now seen as an avoidable consequence of our sexuality. However, it does not stop there; even our idea of sexuality is changing, and this can result in an attitude that disconnects sex from its primary earthly purpose, that being procreation, and its primary spiritual element, the relationship. When built on equality and mutual respect, sex becomes an important aspect of our deepest relationships. Intimacy can build trust and reinforce the love in that relationship. This physical dialogue can also enhance those everyday conversations needed to keep the relationship healthy.

If we are not respectful of the convenience of contraceptives, the effect will likely be that sex is viewed as a form of recreation. The repercussions of this type of attitude in the long term may be sexual irresponsibility, that degrades the meaning and value of the relationships between couples. In the worst case, it can cheapen your partner to nothing more than an object of self-enjoyment or a form of entertainment. One could say that this mindset is not new, but one could also argue that the acceptance of this behavior has been bolstered and grown since the introduction of contraceptives. The consequences of our open sexuality may have been minimized by contraceptives, but our responsibility toward sex and each other should never be compromised.

In so many ways, our modern principles and our present-day ideas seem to emphasize the wrong approaches in life. Perhaps this is partly because so many more things in our day-to-day life distract us. Probably too, it is because some people just do not know how to have a stable and loving relationship within their own family, or more importantly, with themselves.

Our view of sex is one factor that may affect our future. Today's modern culture places a high value on success, but this ideal seems increasingly measured by the fulfillment of self and gaining monetary wealth. Almost to the same degree, our modern culture pushes individuality. This is most likely a side effect of our need to compete in a highly competitive world, or it may just derive from our own vanity. It could also be attributed to our self-centered desire to be unique, to stand out in a world that is driven by conformity.

Career success, wealth, and individuality at the expense of family can be a misguided idea that disconnects us from the real substance, the real happiness in life, and that is family. We have a lifetime to build a career. In fact, most people will likely have multiple careers over their lifetime. The careers and the jobs will come and go, but our family is the one constant in our lives. As such, this should be our primary goal and one of our highest priorities. True success must also be measured through our commitment to family.

For the most part, there is nothing wrong with the pursuit of our own success or working to ensure the success of our children. But our modern ideas of success have become a double-edged sword, a paradigm that stems from within the family but at the same time works against the concept of family. When parents push their children down any narrowly defined path, there can be unintended repercussions if all involved are too focused on that endeavor. This is especially true if it puts marriage and family a distant second in our lives and leaves a promise unfulfilled. There is no long-term success in life if it does not include family, and there is no more significant measure of wealth than that which lives in your grandchildren.

It could be said that within our modern high-tech lifestyle, we are creating a highly educated and intensely dedicated generation motivated by putting their self-serving interests first without much thought about how it affects their future. When given a choice, they will not only take the path of least effort but the way that seems to allow them to fulfill the highest number of their own needs and desires, regardless of the true cost. For those living this self-centered lifestyle, they should stop and reflect on this. Sometimes, life is not about getting what you think you deserve or being exactly what you want. Nor is it about compromise or even settling. Sometimes it is simply about loving or learning to value what you already have. Each of us needs to understand that it is not what is on the outside that defines you. What matters is the integrity of your inner-self. That which we find on the outside is superficial and is often driven by vanity. Dwelling too much on those external details drives us towards obsessiveness. This can overshadow the noble soul, stifling your happiness by pushing you off the path of a more holistic and genuine lifestyle.

The compounded effects of our modern lifestyles seem to be colliding at the intersection of our ever-increasing selfishness, our misguided view of success, our obsessive quest for uniqueness, and our eroding sexual values. Without a responsible mindset and the presence of healthy relationships, there is no control—no stoplight, so to speak—and people will continue to collide and to be hurt, abused, or exploited in this intersection. We all need to be mindful of the choices we make for ourselves and of the values we pass on to children. The choices we make today could be failing our children, eroding our family values, and to a greater extent, wearing holes in the very fabric of our society.

When discussing the different factors that are affecting our society, one cannot address them without touching on homosexuality, which some might say, in the greater scheme of nature, is an unsustainable behavior within any species. To be fair, the same question can be asked of couples who have chosen to remain childless or individuals who prefer to stay single. The first question is: Does this equate to genetic waste, or does this merely fall within an acceptable surplus in humanity? The defining question then becomes: Can our human population support these individuals and more importantly, accept this behavior?

Generally, in terms of our earthly nature and for many people, the answers to the first questions would likely be yes and yes. Nevertheless, when we look at it through the spiritual side of our nature, which allows us to put aside the first earthly questions, then the answers to the defining questions should be yes and yes. What is important is that we all must put peace first in our lives and remember that we are all equal and that each and every life is sacred. When we measure these questions through the simplest of truths, we can then accept or at least respect the choices these people have made, regardless of whether we agree or not. Even if their decisions might have taken them out of a direct contribution to the future, they still have gifts to give that can help fulfill a legacy to our greater humanity.

What it really comes down to, is that it is not so much about sex or the kind of sexual attraction we have for others. Sex is, really, nothing more than just a sideshow to the main event under the big top. The greatest show is the one being played out in the center ring, and that is the relationship. Despite our preoccupation and obsession with sex, our sexuality does not define our relationships. It is the relationship, not sex, which fulfills our need for companionship and provides long-term happiness. The fundamentals of any healthy relationship are always the same, regardless of who is involved in that relationship.

We all must remember to let God be the judge, especially of those who have accepted and are living their lives by the simplest of truths. This must be acknowledged because we as a people cannot hope to understand the real cost and the ramifications of our intolerance. At the same time, we cannot underestimate the ripple effects that our selfish actions can have within our society, especially when it concerns our views toward sex, relationships, and family, or what consequences our modern conveniences and ideologies may have on the future of all humanity.

The fact is, most modern, industrialized countries have declining birth rates. As a result, these countries have become heavily invested in a small family. This may be because of the high cost of having children and raising a family. Though, if we are not careful, a low birth rate in combination with all these other factors, which are mostly built around individual needs, self-achievement, and self-expression above family, could have devastating effects on our future. The collective sum of these factors could result in large segments of humanity traveling down a path to a slow, silent, and insidious form of genocide.

If we are going to embrace smaller families of one or two children, then we need to make it our highest priority that our adult children understand the critical importance of honoring the promise, by starting their own family. A parent's job is never really done, so they should never stop inspiring and supporting their adult children, as much as they can, with this endeavor. We all must understand the importance of our goal as an adult: to raise children who are ready for their ultimate purpose, that of being a parent. We honor our grandparents by fulfilling the legacy of our parents, and this is achieved through our own journey down the path of parenthood.

In the end, we must understand that our children are our only legacy. They are our future. Yes, parenthood will be the most challenging task we will ever face because it requires so many sacrifices. It calls for a commitment to give of yourself, to look beyond the self, and to prepare the next generation for their role in life. Hopefully, we can accomplish this without losing too much of ourselves as individuals in the process.

Now more than ever, as a global village, we have to be conscious of our actions. This is especially true in the context of our misguided views of success and wealth in combination with our obsessive preoccupation with self and uniqueness. We also need to be conscious of how our selective control over our reproduction and our declining respect for sex, relationships, and family will ultimately affect our task of building tomorrow.

Walking out of the Dark: Part Five

Nature of Love

Silent, without notice, Life's Promise falls to the ground,
invisible and undisturbed.

Slowly, a Seed's Trust reaches out,
finding the fond embrace of earth, solid and assured.

Whispers, the Soil's Soul murmurs encouragement,
extruding its essence, nurturing and guidance.

Unwinding, in time a Sapling's Dialogue grows steady
in the mud, unassuming and enlightening.

Singing, a melody in the Spring's Tone resonates,
stirring and reassuring.

Humming, the triumph in the Summer's Harmony swells,
warm and contented.

Golden, the Autumn's Love Song echoes
in the honeymoon harvest, abundant and pervasive.

Bleakness, a bitter cold discord in the Winter's Exchange,
forceful and contested.

Awareness, an understanding of the Season's Rhythm
and Energy's Balance, analyzed, and negotiated.

Reaching, the canopy of the Tree's Conversation reveals
the Root's Cause, forgiveness and forgiven.

The Simplest of Truths

*Soaring, upon wings the Curiosity's Discovery brings
Tomorrow's Potential, recycling and renewing.*

*Fulfillment, from every corner Perception's Viewpoint tempers
Need's Desire, respect and companionship.*

*Sharing, the energy between Spirit's Marriage and
Earth's Family entwine, encompassing and unbroken.*

*Growing, the impact of Peace's Relationship and
Time's Honesty bound together, integrity and wisdom.*

*Enlightenment, the nature of Love's Legacy holds
Truth's Simplicity by a promise, received and given.*

Arthur woke from a restless sleep. It was the middle of the night, but his mind was spinning with energy as if anger, fear, and frustration were all rolled into one. He shifted to his left side and tried to relax, but his body seemed to be vibrating or pulsing with the same energy. He closed his eyes and tried doing the breathing exercise Mairwyn had suggested.

He was so tried but kept to the deep breathing. Was it six or was it seven days now? He could not remember. His trouble sleeping had started to affect every part of his life. At first, Mairwyn did not have much sympathy for him. She was in the last few weeks of her fourth pregnancy, and at first, her only reply was, "Welcome to my world." However, as his sleepless nights continued, she too became concerned. Arthur felt himself relax a bit and kept up the breathing exercises.

He snapped awake again, mind and body buzzing. Somewhere in mid-thought, he had drifted back to sleep, but it did not last. He rolled onto his back and lay staring at the blackness that was the ceiling. He had felt terrible when he crawled into bed just a few hours ago. He typically loved spending the evening with the kids, but his increasingly quick temper was getting the better of him. Kaisa and Izrik were getting weary of their grumpy daddy, and poor little Arthur just started crying when he went to tuck him into bed.

He started the breathing exercise again, but his thoughts turned around and around, trying to figure out what was causing his insomnia. His diet had not changed, and there wasn't anything overly stressful going on at the inn or the brickworks. His relationship with Mairwyn was solid, outside of the fact that she was nine months pregnant and at times very irritable. With the general's death, most of the major fighting in the war had ceased. That and the pressures from his local representative obligations were significantly reduced. Yet something had to be affecting him. He started thinking about the possible causes, anything he might be overlooking.

Arthur snapped awake again. "Damn it," he whispered under his breath and then quickly rolled out of bed. Maybe I should try one of the comfortable wing chairs in the office, he thought. He turned to grab a pillow and one of the blankets from the bed. Even in the dark, he could tell Mairwyn was not there. He sprinted out of their room, down the hallway to the privy. She was not there, but from that vantage point, he could see the light in the kitchen. In a dozen long strides, he was in the kitchen. Mairwyn was leaning over the sink.

"Are you all right, Wyn?" he asked as he walked up behind her.

"Ha," she half laughed, half grunted. "Aunt Kaisa was right; you do have a way about you to show up when you're needed most." The sentence came out in three ragged gasps. "My water broke, and I was going to come and get you once this contraction stopped." Again, the sentence came out in three gasps.

Arthur grabbed a clean towel from the shelf, wet it in the other sink, and wiped the sweat from Mairwyn's brow. When her white-knuckled grip on the edge of the sink started to ease, he helped her straighten up. "Now, let's get you back into bed, and I will make a call for Dr. Yangre." He put one arm around her waist, she put an arm over his shoulders, and they set off to their bedroom.

"He better get here quick; I think this little one is in a hurry to arrive," she said in a much more normal voice.

After getting Mairwyn settled in bed, he went to the second floor and woke Olena. To his surprise, she seemed to come awake at once. With much clarity and intuition, she seemed to know exactly what was happening and knew what she needed to do and set off to be with Mairwyn. From there, he peeked in on all three kids and then headed back downstairs to the kitchen. He set a kettle of water on the stove to boil and then started brewing a pot of coffee.

As Arthur was adding the coffee grounds, a thought crossed his mind. Maybe I am drinking too much coffee throughout the day? He made a mental note to try to limit his coffee to mornings only.

After calling the physician, he sent the inn's night clerk to the road to wait and watch for him. Arthur then returned to the kitchen. When the coffee was finished brewing, he poured himself a cup and went back to the lobby to wait for Dr. Yangre.

His thoughts returned to the day, in the not so distant past, when Dr. Yangre and his son Elias had walked into the lobby and back into his life. Absently, he thought that he was likely sitting in the same chair that day as well. He remembered the day clearly because it had only been a day or two before Mairwyn went into labor with their first child, Kaisa. Only later did he realize how incredibly fortunate they had been with Dr. Yangre's auspicious arrival. Arthur closed his eyes and that day's events raced through his mind.

* * *

Arthur was sitting in the lobby talking and laughing with Olena, a couple of their guests, and a few local friends who always seemed to gather in the lobby in the late afternoon. When two men walked in, the spirited conversation quickly faded.

"Welcome," said Olena from behind the front desk. "How can I help you?"

"Well," said the older gentleman rather hesitantly. "I'm looking for Naomi. Would she still be the proprietor of this inn?"

"No," said Arthur somewhat harshly. Yet Arthur felt there was something oddly familiar in the way the older man carried himself. His posture seemed solid and assured, but his attitude was humble. Softening his tone, Arthur continued. "Naomi passed away quite some time ago."

"Oh, I see," said the gentleman softly.

The man seemed to Arthur to deflate slightly. His gaze drifted briefly toward the floor as he reached up and removed his hat.

"May I inquire about two relatives of hers, Zachary and Kaisa?" asked the gentleman.

At first, Arthur was hard pressed to find any words, and in the growing silence, the small group that was gathered in the lobby started to drift out of the inn or back up to their rooms. Arthur looked at both men, his thoughts turning slowly around how and when these two men had come to know his mum as well as his aunt and uncle. The whole time the younger man was staring intensely at Arthur.

"They, too, have passed on," he finally said in a soft voice. "Now, may I ask your names and why you are looking for my mum and my aunt and uncle?"

The younger man's face broke out in a big smile. "I knew it was you, Arthur."

The older man cleared his throat. "I am Dr. Yangre, and as you have now likely guessed, this is my son, Elias."

Arthur crossed the lobby and shook the doctor's hand. "Good to see you again, Dr. Yangre." He then turned to Elias. "I should have known straight away who I was dealing with by that mischievous gleam in your eyes." Arthur reached to shake Elias's hand, but at the last moment, the two quickly went through the motions of their secret childhood handshake, which ended with them leaning in and vigorously pounding each other on the back.

"So what brings you back to this sleepy corner of the world?"

Dr. Yangre cleared his throat again. "First, I must say that I am very sorry to hear about your mother's passing. She was a good-hearted person, and so too were your aunt and uncle." After a rather awkward silence, the doctor continued. "I guess you could say that we are here for lodging. We are in need of a temporary place to stay while I look for a place to rent or buy. I am not, should I say, comfortable living on the coast any longer, and your sleepy little town tucked up in this mountain valley seemed to be calling me."

"So we're to be neighbors again?" Arthur's question had been directed at both men, but he had been looking at Elias.

Elias's smile faded. "No," he replied. "I am only here until I can get Dad comfortably settled and then I need to return to the coast and make arrangements to transport his belongings here. After that, it's back to my army unit." Elias's mood seemed to darken. "Tensions with the general and his government are running very high along the coast, and it was my hope that dad would be safer here." Elias smiled again. "Knowing you're here, Arthur, is an enormous relief."

Just then, Olena's excited voice could be heard drifting down the hallway, and the three men turned to look. A second later, Olena came rushing into the lobby with Mairwyn in tow. "Mairwyn, Mairwyn, this is Dr. Yangre. He is the wonderful doctor that helped deliver you."

* * *

"Arthur, Arthur, wake up!" Someone was lightly shaking his shoulder.

Arthur woke confused and struggled to orient himself. "Damn it," he cursed silently, "I must have fallen asleep again." Dr. Yangre was standing over him. Recovering some of his senses, he stood up and shook the physician's hand. "Thank you for coming," Arthur said, "at this early hour." He wanted to say "so quickly," but Arthur was not sure how long he had slept. "Mairwyn thinks the baby is in a hurry to arrive."

"Babies set their own schedule," said Dr. Yangre. "We just learn to accommodate them and help them along when it's needed. Now, let's go see how Mairwyn is doing, shall we?"

Both men started making their way to the small two-story apartment that was attached to the back of the inn. "Have I ever told you how grateful and thankful I am that you chose to move back here when you did? I mean, if you had not been here..." Arthur swallowed hard against a wave of sadness that threatened to overwhelm him, and somehow he managed to say, "I might have lost Mairwyn and little Kaisa."

Dr. Yangre stopped and put his hand on Arthur's shoulder. "But I was here that day, Arthur, and everything turned out fine. Don't dwell on things that didn't happen. Be joyful in what you have today. You have a woman who loves you deeply, and you have three wonderful expressions of that love you and Mairwyn share. Soon a fourth. Any man should be so blessed."

The physician moved his hand from Arthur's shoulder, and he looked away, gazing off down the hallway, his body slumped ever so slightly. "Have I ever told you how sorry I am about leaving you and your mum all those years ago?" The physician's gaze fell back on Arthur. "I did very much love your mum, but I was a hard-headed fool then, too proud to admit my mistakes. I didn't fully realize what I was walking away from at the time."

Dr. Yangre stared off down the hallway again. "Lately, I find myself wondering," the physician said, "if I had been a better man then, I could have made a difference. I could have made a difference in Naomi's life. I regret that I didn't try to stay in touch with her, to know what was going on here, and I also regret that it took me so long to find the courage to come back."

"But you did come back, and you have made a difference here. Not just for Mairwyn and me, but for many people in this area."

"Thank you, Arthur. I'm glad you think so." The physician turned back to Arthur. "You know, if you and Mairwyn need anything—anything—just say so, and I will do what I can to help."

Dr. Yangre's face broke out in a big smile, and he threw his arm over Arthur's shoulders and gave him a quick shake. "Now, let's go welcome your little one into the world."

Both men continued down the hallway. "How's Mairwyn's studying coming along?" asked the physician as they entered the bedroom. He did not wait for an answer but strode over to Mairwyn.

"My dear girl, if I asked you a question, would you be able to answer?" asked Dr. Yangre.

Mairwyn was in the middle of a contraction and could only shake her head. She was standing and leaning heavily on the back of a chair. Olena was next to Mairwyn, talking her through the contraction.

"Your contractions are quite strong, then," he said. After the contraction had faded, he added, "So you have been walking in between your contractions? When did your water break?"

Olena started to answer, but Mairwyn interrupted her. "He wants to hear it from me, Mom. I think he is trying to test me." She looked up and glared at the physician. "My water broke about two hours ago, with contractions coming about six minutes apart. My contractions are now much stronger and are coming about every three minutes. The baby has started to drop, but I don't think he or she has dropped fully yet." While she talked, Olena was walking her around the bedroom.

"Mairwyn," Dr. Yangre said in an apologetic tone, "I am not trying to test your knowledge or your patience. Although I must say that you will make a fine general practitioner one day. A physician needs to be calm and remain clear of thought, even under stress. You are proving that quality this morning." He looked toward Arthur, knowing all too well that he had initially opposed the idea of Mairwyn studying to become a doctor.

Arthur locked eyes with Mairwyn and then gave her a wink. "I will do all I can to help her achieve her goals, Doctor. She has my full support."

"Good to hear, Arthur, very good indeed. Now, help me with that small table," said Dr. Yangre. He and Arthur then moved the small side table closer to the bed. The physician then laid out a small white towel and carefully arranged items from his medical bag. Once he was done, he turned back to Mairwyn. "So, my dear girl, since you gave me such a good assessment of your condition, what is your estimation on when the next stage of labor will start?"

Mairwyn and Olena were still walking around the bedroom. "That will depend on how dilated and effaced I am. I am hoping you can tell me in the next few minutes that I am around eight centimeters and..." Mairwyn could not finish her sentence, as the next contraction had started.

"Olena, Arthur, help her to bed after this contraction is over. I am just going to wash up. I will be right back, Mairwyn; hang in there." At that, Dr. Yangre walked out of the bedroom.

Over the next few hours, Arthur was so wholly absorbed in encouraging and supporting Mairwyn, he had forgotten how tired he was. By midmorning, Mairwyn had delivered a healthy baby girl. After Arthur had spent some time holding his tiny newborn daughter and had been assured that Mairwyn and baby were fine, both Olena and Dr. Yangre sent him off to get some rest.

He ended up in one of the comfortable wing chairs next to the fireplace in the inn's office. Once he had his feet propped up on a matching footstool and had covered himself with the blanket, he had discarded so many long hours ago, he quickly fell asleep.

"Arthur." Someone was shaking him. "Arthur." The voice had an urgent tone to it.

"What?" said Arthur irritably as his eyes flew open. "Is Mairwyn okay? Is it the baby?

"Yes and no," said Parisch, who had been filling in at the front desk for Olena. "Mom and baby are doing just fine, but there is a man who claims to be a friend of yours and some other stern-looking men in the lobby. They want to speak to you. I tried telling them that you weren't available, but they insisted I find you."

Arthur slowly got up and neatly folded the blanket and draped it over the back of the chair. With a quick glance in the mirror that hung in the office, he smoothed out his hair. He thought that he really did feel better than he actually looked. Only then did he follow Parisch out to the lobby.

From near the front door, Harmon, an old friend from his days in the Revolutionary Army, greeted him. "Arthur, my friend," he said and then hesitated. "I was going to say you looked good and haven't changed a bit, but if you don't mind me saying so, you look terrible. Is everything okay?"

"Like I told you earlier," Parisch said in a rather testy voice from the front desk, "his wife just had a baby—"

Arthur cut in. "That's okay, Parisch. I'm fine and certainly up for entertaining an old friend and a few guests."

Harmon glared at the clerk. "May we speak with you, Arthur, in private? This is rather important."

"My office is just around the corner, gentlemen. This way," he said, leading the men out of the lobby and closing the office door after they had all filed in.

*   *   *

Hours later, Olena found Arthur alone in the inn's office, sitting at his desk. His elbows were planted on the desktop, and his chin was resting on the back of his crossed fingers as he stared blankly down at a packet of papers.

"Are you all right, Arthur? You look even more tired than you did this morning. Were you not able to get some sleep?"

"I did get a couple of good hours in before Parisch woke me," said Arthur.

"I gave that man explicit instructions that no one was to disturb you," she protested.

"At any rate, I don't think Harmon was going to take no for an answer, even if it had been you behind the front desk today." Arthur was going to add that things had come to a point where he had very nearly been arrested but decided against it. At that moment, he felt he really needed to talk with Mairwyn, and the sooner, the better.

Olena just looked at him, waiting for him to give her all the details. When he did not, she merely stated that dinner was ready and that the kids were waiting for him in the kitchen.

Arthur was instantly on his feet. "You know, Olena, I just realized that I have not had anything to eat all day. I didn't even think about breakfast this morning with the baby coming and all. Then I slept through lunch, and this afternoon brought the damn meeting with Harmon. I'm starving."

"Well, no wonder you look so terrible—go eat," she said, and she shooed him out of the office.

As soon as Arthur walked into the kitchen, three kids surrounded him. Kaisa and Izrik were excited about the news of their baby sister, and both started talking to him at the same time.

Little Arthur just wanted to be held. After hugs and kisses on the forehead for each, he scooped little Arthur up and herded the other two over to the table. Just after they had settled in at the table, Olena came into the kitchen. The inn's cook, Nelka, had already prepared a tray for Mairwyn. As if on cue, Nelka handed Olena the tray, and she swept back out of the kitchen, on her way back to Mairwyn.

"Based on the smell," said Arthur to the kids, "I think Nelka has prepared a special dinner for us."

Before they started, Arthur asked Nelka to join them. When she began to refuse, he insisted. During dinner, Kaisa proudly announced that she had set the table all by herself. Nelka nodded at Arthur and thanked Kaisa for all her help in the kitchen.

"Nelka," said Kaisa, "how did you learn to cook so good?"

"Yeah, how?" added Izrik.

Arthur remembered Nelka's story from a letter his aunt had sent him while he was still at the university. She had caught Nelka eating food from the trash bin behind the inn and offered her a real meal. Aunt Kaisa had kept up a conversation while she finished cooking. When Nelka asked about how she knew which herbs and spices to use, his aunt offered to teach her how to cook. In exchange, Nelka agreed to help Aunt Kaisa with the grocery shopping.

Nelka looked at Arthur as if looking for permission. He nodded. "I learned to cook from your great Aunt Kaisa," said Nelka. "The very lady that you were named after," Nelka said as she leaned over and tapped one finger on little Kaisa's nose. "She was such a great lady."

"Why, I remember when I was first learning to cook, I couldn't have been much older than you, my dear girl. Your great aunt and I would talk about all sorts of things. She used to say that cooking was a lot like life—some things are sweet, some are bitter. Other things are sour, and still, others are spicy, but they all have their own place in the kitchen. Sometimes she would just say that life is like good food—there's always more to it than you think. She would say it's about the preparations and the right proportions, about moderation and how you lay it out on the plate, and it is about enjoying it."

"I like cake," said Izrik, "Whiff lots of frosting."

Both Arthur and Nelka chuckled. "I do too," said Arthur as he reached over and ruffled Izrik's hair.

Little Arthur, who was sitting on Arthur's lap, turned to look up at him. "Cake?" he asked.

Arthur ruffled his hair, too. "No cake tonight, buddy."

"Dad, what's the baby's name going to be?" asked Kaisa. "And when can we see Mom?"

Olena, who had just returned to the kitchen with the empty tray, answered one of the questions for him. "You can see both of them in a little while...after you finish what's on your plates. So get eating."

Nelka had risen from the table as soon as Olena walked into the kitchen and retrieved the tray from her. She deposited it in the large sink, made up a plate for Olena, and then returned to being busy in the kitchen.

While the two older kids feverishly finished what was left of their meal, Arthur helped little Arthur with whatever he was willing to eat. In between feeding little Arthur, he managed to finish everything on his plate, too.

"Dad, what's the baby's name going to be?" asked Kaisa again.

"Your mom and I discussed a few names, but we haven't come up with one we like yet."

Kaisa frowned. "Da-ad, you gotta pick one. I don't think I can fall asleep tonight if she doesn't have a name." She rolled her eyes, folded her arms across her chest, and slumped back into the chair.

"Well, you know, when Nelka was retelling stories about Aunt Kaisa, she made me think about something my aunt told me once. I had forgotten about it until now. I don't remember exactly when it was or how old I was, but I remember walking into this kitchen one morning. My aunt was sitting at this very table, and she looked tired, but it wasn't until I got closer that I saw that she had been crying. I remember asking her what's wrong. She just smiled at me and said she was just missing her sisters Naomi and Itanni. Naomi is your grandma, my mum, but I had never heard the name Itanni before or since then either.

"So, what would you think about the name Itanni?" asked Arthur.

"I like it," and "It's good," said Kaisa and Izrik at the same time. Even Olena agreed.

Little Arthur smiled and said, "Tanni" and then stuffed another bite of food in his mouth.

"Well, then, let's wash up and go see what your mom thinks."

Once everyone was washed up, Olena grabbed little Arthur and carried him out of the kitchen, heading to Arthur and Mairwyn's bedroom. She was followed closely by the other two. Arthur left the kitchen as well but made a quick detour to the inn's office to pick up the packet of papers Harmon had left.

Once he had arrived in the bedroom, he found the three kids gathered around their mom. She was propped up, sitting up at the head of the bed with the baby cradled in her arms. Olena was standing at the end of the bed, and all had big smiles on their faces.

Arthur found a spot on the edge of the bed. No sooner had he sat down than little Arthur climbed onto his lap. He pointed to the baby. "Baby Tanni," he said.

"You never told me you had an Aunt Itanni," said Mairwyn.

"Insofar as I can recall, Aunt Kaisa only ever mentioned her once, and I know nothing more about her. I'm not entirely sure why or what made me remember that specific moment with my aunt during dinner tonight. So, what do you think? Do you like the name Itanni?"

"I love the name, Arthur. It's the perfect name for this little girl," replied Mairwyn.

It was not too much longer before Olena shooed the children out of the bedroom with a promise that she would read them a book before bedtime. Before she left, she reminded Mairwyn and Arthur that Dr. Yangre would be stopping by soon to check up on his patients.

As soon as the door closed, Arthur pulled the packet of papers from his pocket. At the same time, Mairwyn asked, "What did Harmon want? Did he bring news from the capital?"

"Here, let me hold my little girl again, and you might want to read this." He laid the packet next to Mairwyn and then carefully scooped the baby out of her arms. Arthur paced the room for a short while. Baby Itanni had opened her eyes and was staring intensely at Arthur through squinted, slow-blinking eyes. Arthur gently stroked her cheek, and she let out a mighty yawn, which made Arthur yawn. He then sat down in the big overstuffed chair by the cradle and talked softly to his daughter.

From his vantage point, Arthur could tell that the more Mairwyn read, the more agitated she became. "How can they do this?" she finally said. "There are other people in this country that call it home than just the damn faithful. This is wrong Arthur—almost immoral. This proclamation is a huge betrayal of the people, of all the people who fought and supported the effort to rid this country of the general and his cronies that don't happen to be a part of The Faithful."

"I know," said Arthur. "I told Harmon as much and was near arrested for it."

"Arrested? On what kind of charges, and by whose authority?"

"By the authority of the grand priest, and treason was mentioned. What was even more frightening was that those men held no regard for my rights. If it hadn't been for Harmon asking for a private conversation with me to try and convince me of the 'errors in my thinking,' I would not be here now."

"What!" Mairwyn's voice was panicked. She was scared.

Arthur quickly continued. "At some point, Harmon told me that if I were to be arrested, he could not guarantee my safety. When Harmon did finally leave, he left extremely disappointed because I did the only thing my conscience would allow me to do. I resigned my position as this regional representative, but that seemed to appease the others."

Mairwyn just stared at him angrily.

"I'm honestly not so sure if my resignation wasn't their objective from the beginning. Maybe Harmon or the other men thought by convincing me to join their cause, it would influence others in this region. One thing is for certain—this was a win for them either way," finished Arthur.

In the long silence that followed, Arthur got up and carefully laid a sleeping Itanni in the crib. The silence was only broken by a soft knock on the door.

"Dr. Yangre here; may I come in?"

"Please do," said Arthur.

When the good doctor opened the door, he immediately noticed the tear streaks down Mairwyn's cheeks. He turned and looked at Arthur, who was still standing next to the cradle. "Is there something wrong, or is this a bad time for a checkup on Mom and baby?" he asked. A knot formed in his belly. Arthur and Mairwyn were like family to him, and he did not like to see them upset.

"No, please stay," said Arthur. "But I have received some news from Harmon today, news that will likely affect you and Elias, too."

"Yes," said Mairwyn, "you need to read this for yourself." At that point, she unfolded the packet and offered it to the doctor.

The doctor was standing when he started to read the proclamation. By the time he had finished, he was sitting on the edge of the bed. His reaction was very much like Mairwyn's, even as Arthur recounted the meeting with Harmon.

"So they just let you resign?" asked the doctor.

"Sort of," Arthur replied.

"What do you mean by 'sort of' Arthur?" said Mairwyn.

"They want a signed resignation letter by tomorrow morning. Evidently, Harmon and the other men are leaving first thing in the morning and want my letter on the front desk by then."

"Where are they now?" asked the doctor.

"On the second floor of the inn," said Arthur. "I gave them a free night. Didn't think they would pay anyway. Parisch is keeping an eye on them."

"In light of this news, and if you don't mind, I would like to get started on Mom-and-baby checkups. I'm not trying to change the subject, but I really do think I want to try to get in touch with Elias as soon as possible. My people along the coast are an independent lot, and I'm afraid of how this proclamation will be received there."

Arthur excused himself before Dr. Yangre started the check-ups. He stopped by the inn's office and retrieved the resignation letter he had written hours earlier. He slowly read it a couple more times and then signed it. He then dropped it by the front desk, with instructions on who would be looking for it in the morning. When he finally returned to Mairwyn, Dr. Yangre had already left.

"I think Dr. Yangre is really scared for the safety of this son, Arthur," said Mairwyn.

"Yes, I sensed that, too. I think today's news has rattled the good doctor down to his very core."

"It has rattled more than just the doctor," she said.

Arthur sat down on the edge of the bed and sighed. "I wrote my resignation letter earlier today. I have now signed it and left it at the front desk."

"We're going to be okay, Arthur, aren't we?" said Mairwyn.

"I hope so, Wyn," he replied. Arthur yawned, stretched, and then let his breath out slowly. "Wyn," he said, "Why is it that when each of our children was born, something out of the ordinary happened?"

"What do you mean, Arthur?"

"When Kaisa was born, I nearly lost you both. If Dr. Yangre hadn't been here...I don't even want to think about it, because I don't know what I would have done without you. Then before the shock of all that had worn off, you started..."

"Talking about wanting to become a doctor," Mairwyn finished the sentence for him. "Arthur, I thought I was going to die the day I gave birth to Kaisa, but Dr. Yangre kept promising me everything would be fine and said to stay focused on his voice. Ever since then, I am grateful for each day, and from then on, I knew I wanted to do more with my life. I want to be a doctor, Arthur—one like Dr. Yangre."

"I know," said Arthur. "I knew I was selfish at that time, mostly because I wanted to keep you close, so nothing bad could happen to you again. Even though I have said it before, I'm sorry for not supporting you from the start."

"You are an amazing man, Arthur; I knew at the time you would come around sooner or later, but to your credit, you did sooner than even I thought you would."

"Thanks," said Arthur. "I think, during that time, you had more trust in me than I did in myself."

"Anyway, back to my original point," he continued. "All of that happened just when Kaisa was born. On the very day Izrik was born, I was appointed the Mayor of our fair town, which threw a completely new layer of chaos into our lives. When little Arthur came along, the war with the general had just started, and I ended up being appointed as one of the regional representatives for the newly formed coalition. Being away from the four of you was one of the hardest things that I've had to face in my life. Now today, that little girl"—and Arthur pointed to the cradle—"has been born, and I learn that the alliance that so many people have been working on, for the future of this country, has been completely betrayed by that the so-called Faithful." Arthur's voice dropped to a mere whisper. "What kind of life will I be able to give that little girl over there, or for that matter, any of our children?"

"We will raise our children to have respect for others and to treat people fairly and honestly," Mairwyn said. "We will teach them how to live their lives with integrity and, hopefully, show them how to make wise decisions for themselves now and later in their life."

"Will that be enough?" asked Arthur.

"I don't know, Arthur. All we can do is our level best for them. Now, go say goodnight to Kaisa, Izrik, and little Arthur for me. Then come straight back. Today's events have taken a toll on me, and more than ever, I just need you to be near me.

So each time I wake up, I will know you are still here, safe by my side."

Arthur went and said goodnight to the kids and then talked briefly with Olena. He followed his usual bedtime routine by first walking around the inn. He then stopped by the front desk to speak with Parisch, who refused to leave until certain guests had checked out. Only then did he make his way back to Mairwyn. Once in bed, Mairwyn rolled onto her side, slipped one arm around his chest, and was asleep. Even though baby Itanni woke them every few hours, Arthur still had his best night of rest in over a week.

Section 6

Living Choices

God does not have a fixed plan for each of us. God only provides us with the direction, but our path is not always straight or even well-defined. We make our own choices, and we wander aimlessly. We lose the trail or linger longer than we should at certain points along our way. When we find ourselves at those crossroads in life, we may stop to question which is the right road. But there is not always going to be an obvious right or wrong choice, though there will often be a choice between an easy path to travel and another, more demanding path. Regardless of the direction we choose to take or feel forced to make, God's mile markers are always there whether we notice them or not. God may never give us more than we can handle, but the road of life can and often does. When we find and embrace the peace within, when we strive for equality and the sanctity of everyone's life, and when we live our lives with integrity and wisdom, God's mile markers and guideposts will never be hidden from us. It is still our choice to follow them or not.

Whitewash

Long ago, the elder of a remote village became increasingly distraught seeing his grown children, one by one, leaving the village to find a better life elsewhere. No matter what he said, he could not persuade any of them to stay. For him, there was no better place in the world to raise a family. He loved his village and did not want to see all his children leave and for him and his wife be left alone in their old age.

One day, a traveler was passing through town who was known to pass through several times a year. The village elder stopped and asked the man, "What brings you down this road when there are better roads that are more easily traveled?" The man agreed there were better roads but said he enjoyed traveling through the beautiful valley. "And what do you think of our village, then?" asked the elder. To this, the traveler replied, "I'm not saying people here aren't friendly, but as far as I'm concerned, your village is a blight in this beautiful valley. It is dirty, and it stinks. The road through your town is particularly bad, and there is not even an inn to rest for the night. Nothing here makes me want to stop. I just try to pass through as quickly as possible." At that, the traveler scowled and moved on.

The village elder stood on the roadside in shock. He looked around at his village and at the empty road and began to wonder. The more he thought about it, the more he knew what must be done. He called a town meeting to gather support for improving the village. He encouraged villagers to clean up their property and whitewash their homes. With his two remaining sons, they built an oven for firing bricks and tiles, as the village was going to need a cheap, local supply of bricks and tiles to improve their streets. With the first bricks, however, the village elder and his family built an inn. With the help of his wife and youngest daughter, he ran the inn while his remaining sons continued making bricks for the village.

Within the next few years, the dirty village was transformed into a beautiful little town. Now seeing opportunities and a future in the small town, the village elder's three youngest children and much of the village's younger generation chose to stay and build their lives in the village.

As time passed, the little town continued to grow. Many people were attached to the beautiful valley and the quaint small village with its clean yards and neatly painted houses. New residents were encouraged and even eager to build their new, whitewashed homes and keep their property clean. The people were friendly, and it was a good place to call home and raise a family.

A generation passed, and the little town had grown. More and more people from all over the region settled in, but it was increasingly difficult to persuade these newcomers to commit to keeping their property clean and their homes whitewashed. So the newly elected mayor and the town elders drafted an ordinance proclaiming that all houses and businesses should be painted white, and front lawns would be kept mowed and free of trash.

Two more generations passed, and the town had grown. New laws were passed to ensure the city continued to be beautiful and pristine. Anyone found in violation of those laws and ordinances and failed to maintain their property, faced stiff fines, jail time, or public disciplinary measures. In extreme cases, entire families were evicted from their homes, publicly ridiculed and forced to leave town with little more than what they could carry with them. A wall was built around the city proper to keep out any persons deemed unworthy of living in or visiting the well-manicured town. In fact, no other settlements were permitted in the entire valley. Anyone caught squatting in the valley was run off or killed outright.

One day a man stood in the town square, next to the statue of the town's patriarch. He told those gathered there that his great-great-grandfather, the man honored by the statue, would not recognize or even like how his village had changed. He told them that the intent behind what was done long ago was to build opportunities for his children and all the children of the town so they would stay and make their lives in the village he loved.

The crowd became enraged and beat the man. The authorities soon came, and they arrested him. In jail, he was again beaten. Later he was publicly humiliated and whipped in the town square. The mayor and the town council quickly judged the man and his family to be unworthy of being residents of their beautiful town. All their property was confiscated, and a date was set for exile.

As the man and his family were led out of town, someone in the crowd picked up a broken brick and threw it at the man. It was a piece of a brick that the man's family had been making for the town for generations. As the man and the brick fell to the ground, the earth began to shake. The ground shook so hard and so long that many of the buildings in town collapsed. What structures that did not fall in the earthquake burned in the great fire that followed. Except, that is, for one small brick inn near the center of what was once a pristine town.

* * *

Two generations later, a small, dirty village had built up around the old inn, and the people there were friendly. It was a good place to raise a family and buy quality bricks.

The King, the General, and the Priest

Three boys were born in the same year and on the same day. The first was born in the morning, son of the king, a prince, and a child of privilege. The second was born in the afternoon, son of a merchant, and child of opportunities. The third was born in the evening, one of many in an impoverished, rural family, and a child of hardship. These three would grow up very differently, but their destinies would be intertwined.

The child of privilege was raised in all the luxury that royalty could offer, and although he did not want for anything, he was instilled with a sense of honor and duty to throne and country. The child of opportunity was taught that nothing in life was free, but with a good education, the right choices, and a bit of determination, he could achieve any goal. The child of hardship understood from very early on that through hard work and devotion, God would always provide for the faithful, even in the leanest of times.

At the age of twenty-three, the prince's life-changing moment came with his father's sudden death. He was now thrust into the leadership of his country. Though he was now the king, many decisions were made for him, and he resented it. Early on, he vowed to himself to rectify that oversight. By the time, he had reached the twentieth year of his reign he had developed a massive appetite for all the things wealth could buy him. He had set many ambitious plans in motion, such as grand palaces, vacation retreats, government buildings, and massive public-works projects. The latter, however, was never really about the people's needs but rather a reflection of his own wants and desires. He always looked for the next grandest thing. All the while, he was draining the treasury and pushing heavier and heavier taxes on his people. Hidden from view was a growing dark side that brutally suppressed all those who questioned his leadership, disagreed with his decisions or opposed the monarchy. In those long years, the cries of the people grew louder, and the king's response was harsh.

The child of opportunities was taught that the only way to reach your goals in life was to never stop working toward them. He excelled in school and in sports. He understood what it took to get the job done and what was at stake if he did not achieve his goals. His life-changing moment also came at the age of twenty-three; he had just finished university and was preparing to join his father in the family business. A disaster had struck, the family's fortune was gone, and he was forced into military service.

The lessons of his youth served him well, however, and he quickly rose through the ranks. He learned how to connect with the gears of power. He learned to play their game, played it well, and played it to win. He would do anything to make sure opportunities opened up for him. Within the first twenty years of the king's reign, he became the youngest man to achieve the rank of general.

The child of hardship was raised in a simple, hardworking family. However, the hard work and long days came with a price. Half of his siblings died before they were teenagers. It was faith that kept his family going. In his teen years, his parents left him in the care of the local priest, hoping he could take some of the work-load off the old priest's ministry and in the process, lighten the burden on their family. For the young man, these were hard years of toiling under heavy chores. Despite this, he found that discipline, deprivation, and service had their own unique rewards. His life-changing moment came at the age of twenty-three when he received the calling to become a priest.

The devout life was about obedience, respect, restraint, prayer, serving faithfully, and the strictness of routines. This suited him well, and he tirelessly served the priesthood for many years. Through the long years, the young priest's influence and affluence grew, not only among his people but also within the clergy. Within the first twenty years of the king's reign, he was rewarded by being elected and anointed, joining the ranks of the high priests.

At the age of forty-three, all three of these men's lives changed again, intertwined forever by their country's plunge into chaos, destruction, and death. At this time, the king had lost all respect for his subjects. They were merely a means to an end, a tax base, and a near-limitless pool of cheap labor. This state of affairs in the end only benefitted the king. His system of government left most people uneducated, often malnourished, and living well below the poverty level. Those in the middle were barely getting by with what was left after paying their taxes. As long as they paid their taxes, they were, for the most part, left alone.

What started merely as a protest against what the people viewed as the growing disconnect between their hardships and suffering and the opulent lifestyle of the king soon turned into a mass demonstration. The king's response to this was swift and harsh. Many were killed outright in the streets. Some were arrested, dragged away, never to be seen again. This proved to fan the flames of revolution, and it burned like wildfire across a drought-plagued land. As the king cracked down harder and harder on the people, a young general heard their cries for justice.

The general knew all too well the suffering of the people because he had lived through it when his family's business became the target of the king's greed. Because this young general had also been affected by the king's greediness, the people and many of the lower ranks of the military moved to support him. For a year, the bloody civil war raged. The war ended with the king's death and the royal family's exile. The young general had won, and he proclaimed victory with promises to reform every level of government.

For the first couple of years, the general enacted many sweeping changes. Schools and hospitals were built in every corner of the country, and the people were given greater access to both. Even still, this left many of the poorest people and those in remote villages without these essential services. For them the only sure way out of hardship was to join the army—this, at least, guaranteed one hot meal a day. After ten years, the general was still in power, and martial law was still being enforced. The military was now not only the police but also the court of law.

In fact, the general and his chiefs of staff ran every level of government, and it had an influence on every level of society. It was a system that demanded discipline and loyalty, and this was expected from every man, woman, and child. Punishment for petty crimes and crimes against the state was swift and often severe. Long sentences in hard labor camps and executions were common.

Throughout this time, the priest had risen to the very top of his order and had attracted a massive following. Over the next two years, the high priest's message became increasingly critical of the general, the corrupt government, and the rampant cronyism within it. Finally, the general had had enough and ordered the arrest of the high priest, but a massive outpouring of followers gathered and became a human wall, shielding the high priest from the general's military police.

In the end, the high priest was able to slip away, but the price was a river of blood from the bodies of The Faithful that littered the streets. It was the beginning of the end. For the second time in a lifetime, the country was caught up in a brutal civil war. For two years, the battle raged on—two years of suffering, torture, rape, and death at the hands of the armed forces on both sides. At the age of fifty-eight, the general was finally cornered and killed. To the very end, he proclaimed that he was the great hero and liberator of the people.

With the general's death, the high priest quickly seized power and disbanded all levels of the government. He declared that it was too overwhelmingly corrupt to be allowed to continue. The high priest became the grand priest, and his religious order became the new government. Nevertheless, problems started almost immediately. Through a series of proclamations, the grand priest declared that only his true followers could be citizens, and conversion was the only way to gain citizenship. All other religious orders would need special dispensation by the local high priests to practice their faith.

Strict morality laws were enacted for both citizens and noncitizens alike. Punishments doled out for crimes or for not conforming to the moral code were usually public, and The Faithful often received a harsher punishment. Yet the laws were also designed to discourage or limit the religious practices of minority groups. Any practices that the grand priest considered immoral or unorthodox were banned.

As the years passed by, extreme intolerance and deep resentment grew. An outright hatred flared between the people who had at one time stood together, suffered, and shed blood, fighting the despot general. It all boiled over when, at the age of sixty-seven, the grand priest was assassinated. For a third time in a generation, the country was torn apart by war. This time, there seemed to be no limit to the suffering, the cruelty, the senseless slaughter, and the wholesale destruction that gripped the country.

At this time, another man came into prominence, trying to unite and heal the country. He was of simple origins. In fact, he was born shortly after midnight on the same day as the last king, the despot general, and the fundamentalist priest, at an old inn, in a dirty mountain village, and was the son of a brick maker. His defining moment came when he was able to bring all sides together to talk about peace, healing, and the future of the county.

With the help of the brickmaker, honest talks began, and those hardened men and women laid the groundwork for democracy. This was based on the foundation that every person's life was sacred, and it ensured equality and equal representation for all. It provided for everyone's right to an education and to pursue his or her highest potential. It was designed to give any citizen the opportunity to stand up and seek an elected office.

This new government guaranteed the right for everyone to have a voice and the ability to use that voice to question those elected officials. But with this assured right to seek the truth also comes a greater moral responsibility to be truthful and honest in that endeavor. They also made provisions for curbing corruption by limiting the number of terms any elected official could serve.

It was a long road to healing and reconciliation, but over time, many of the hostilities passed away, and a great nation grew out of the ashes of all the firestorms of hate that had come before.

I Am Who Am

Tragically, three friends were killed in an accident. As the mists around them cleared, they found themselves just off a well-worn path. Of the three friends, one was very conservative, an upright, righteous person. Another was very liberal, a free spirit with an open mind. The last was a longtime friend of the other two.

As the three friends walked toward the path, the first friend said to the rest, "Being the most religious and learned about matters of God, I say we should all stick together and go right once we get to the path."

"If you are going right," said the second friend to the first, "I'm going the other way." After a short argument, the second friend turned left and stomped off down the path.

"Well, I guess that's for the best," said the first friend. "Let's get started, and we'll be in heaven before you know it."

As the first friend turned right and started down the path, the third friend sat down along the edge of the trail. "Well, aren't you coming?" asked the first friend of the third.

"I want to take a few minutes to meditate and pray. Maybe God will show me the way," said the third friend.

"You know I'm right. If you don't take too long and hurry after me, you might be able to catch up. If not, I'll be waiting for you when and if you get to heaven."

The third friend sat and watched the other two disappear down their chosen paths and then began to meditate and pray. After a while, a peaceful voice spoke. The third friend's eyes were open. There was no path—only God. The third friend looked around.

"Your friends are not here," said God. "The path that went left led your friend through open prairie. The path gradually widened until there was just the prairie. That prairie eventually stopped at an endless shoreline, where the land dropped steadily and steeply down toward a deep ocean. Many have traveled this path, only to become lost within it, lost within themselves, drifting aimlessly on the current."

"The path that went right led your other friend into the mountains, where very little grows. There is just the path and the rocks on either side. This path divides into two and then never stops branching. Many have traveled this path and become lost on the many trails or lodged between the rocks of the narrowest passages."

"But what of my friends?" asked the third friend.

"Many will learn what you have already uncovered within yourself," said God. "You have looked within yourself and discovered that, despite all that makes you human, I have always been within you and you have embraced me. I have been the calm in the middle of the storm that was your life. I am the peace that strengthens you. I am the source of the love you share with others. I am who am, and you are of me."

And the One said, "I am the Spirit, the Divine, and the Wisdom of the universe. Whatever I will, is created. I am the Spark that sets all in motion, yet I am motionless. I am Peace Eternal, yet I am the Creative Energy flowing through all. I am Indefinable, yet I am defined by Truth. I am Intention, I am Aspiration, and I am Desire."

And the One said, "I am the Creator, the Author, and the Embodiment of the universe. Whatever is willed, I create. I am the Passion that brings forth life, yet I am empty of it. I am Love Unbound, yet I am bound by it. I am the Quintessence, yet I am the Nurturing Grace existing in all. I am Realization, I am Fulfillment, and I am Gratification."

And the One said, "The universe and everything in it is within me; I encompass it entirely. You are but one speck of dust, yet you encompass me entirely. I am beyond the universe, yet I am within you. I exist both within and without at the same time, yet I am simply One. I have always been and will always be."

And the One said, "If you can look and wonder about the world around you, then I have touched you. If you have been loved and have given love in return, I am with you. If you have found a deep peace within yourself and embraced it, you have found me."

"To withhold love and fill your heart with hate is to reject me. To hold onto your anger and hurt someone with it is to reject peace. To be frightened is human, but to let fear rule your life is to mistrust yourself, mistrust me, and ignore peace."

And the One said, "It is as important to forgive as it is to seek forgiveness. For no one can reach final judgment and eternal peace until the debts have been paid and the debts are forgiven."

And the One said, "No one who kills or kills in my name—who takes the life of the innocent—knows me, and their soul will dwell in the sorrow, the pain, and the suffering of all their victims. Alone they will dwell in anguish, crying out for mercy until the souls of all their dead have given them their full forgiveness. The same shall pass to the self-righteous ones who have been cruel, unjust, and unforgiving."

And the One said, "There is only one greater crime against me. That is, to persuade others to die and take the lives of the innocent, all in my name. For those guilty of this, there will be no forgiveness. Their souls will dwell utterly alone; no one will hear their wails, and they will suffer all the pain and grief of their victim's victims until their souls are completely consumed."

Walking Out of the Dark: Part Six

Intertwined

Tangled, life branches out with an essence untamed, intentions and their repercussions grow in every conceivable and unintended direction, Unruly yet Defined.

Woven, strings of impulses spin the choices we make, one thread upon the last with the patterns within the lace not easily discerned, Coarse yet Refined.

Emergent, new variations endlessly bud undeterred, different attitudes often stemming out of the remnants of the roots of older concepts, Diverging and Spreading.

Unforeseen, both the good or careworn decisions intertwine to create a greater whole, an unimagined yet tangible fabric that is easily overlooked, Irregular and Designed.

Stillness, knowing how to pause and observe is to find the bits of our psyche needing groomed or see the weak stems of our persona that need cut, a Perspective in Introspection.

Connections, identifying the varied contours of our thoughts and actions can allow the development of a weave of wisdom that builds our long-term integrity, a Measure in Composure.

Nurtured, grown carefully over time uprightness can provide a kind of spiritual tree to shelter under when the heat of living become overwhelming, Instinctive Unpretentiousness.

Guided, the better choices made today and every day can in time provide a type of spiritual blanket woven to warm the soul from an often-cold world, Analyzed Principles.

Arthur woke, and those old feelings were back again, but now he did not try to push them away. He turned on his side. Mairwyn lay sleeping beside him; she looked so peaceful and beautiful in the early morning light. He thought about how he had almost let her walk out of his life and then pushed that thought away. He thought about his aunt and his uncle. He thought about his mum. They had all loved him, and their love was with him still. Their legacy was a part of the love he shared with Mairwyn, and it was in the love that he was passing on to their four children.

Arthur got up, quickly washed and dressed, and then made his way to the kitchen and brewed a pot of coffee. Mug in hand, he then climbed up the stairs to the roof. This was his time to watch the sunrise over the mountains and take in the beauty and the peace of that moment. It was also a time to be at peace with himself, to contemplate the future and think things through.

Since he had moved back to his village, to the inn, Arthur had learned that true happiness was found in the relationships he formed with others. Not just in the deeper relationships he had with Mairwyn or his children, but also in the everyday friendships, and even with casual acquaintances, if he took the time to talk and to listen.

His mind kept returning to larger issues, and his gaze drifted in the general direction of the capital. He had heard the murmurings of conflict. In some respects, he had perceived it before the death of the general because many of the underlying factors had not really changed. Life under the current government was not any better than when the last king or the general had ruled the country. It lacked the integrity and the wisdom to do justice for all levels of society, and it was still rife with its own style of corruption. Arthur did not believe that the fragments of the old coalition that was still the main opposition to the current government could do any better if things did change.

Without true equality and equal representation for all, without genuine respect for each other or a fair system of governing, and without any real willingness to see beyond itself, the current government would continue to be ineffective for many portions of the country. The same age-old problems were still there— issues that were already threatening to tear the country down again.

Arthur thought back to just before the long two-year conflict to overthrow the general had started. At the time, he had only recently been appointed the mayor, mainly because the town had been growing and prospering again, and it needed leadership. He had been the first person in a generation, since the great earthquake, to hold that position. In fact, many of the towns and villages in the mountain regions were experiencing growth. Some more than others, but generally, all were prospering.

Initially, the mountain region benefitted from the changes the general had set in motion at the start of his regime. The prosperity continued even though the government aid was short-lived. The mountain region was just too far removed from the capital to secure continued support or gain much notice by the general and his government.

Arthur was one of only a few people who understood that the region's continued growth was due, in part, to the influx of people fleeing the corruption of the more densely populated farmlands nearer the capital. People came because they believed the mountains offered a safe haven and because it was relatively removed from the rest of the country. In return, those people had brought with them their skills, their businesses, and their wealth.

Arthur's thoughts turned again to the time during the war with the general. It had been one of the most rewarding times in his life but also one of the most difficult. He had worked hard to gain the trust of the people of the mountains, and he had worked even harder to keep the war out of it. They did their part, though indirectly, to support those who fought against the general. The mountains were a place for the wounded to heal, and a place where refugees could feel safe.

Looking back, he knew he could not have really done anything differently. He was not trying to become the voice of his people. The other village elders and mayors came to him for advice, and they set him on that particular path. Most had agreed that the right thing to do was to support the so-called faithful in their fight against the general, and the mountain region was not the only group to do so. Through those hard years, Arthur came to know many people from the many different regions, ethnic groups, and faiths of his country, many of whom he still considered his friends.

Whenever Arthur let his thoughts wander down this particular path, they always seemed to drift back to what later became known as the Betrayal of The Faithful. This event came in the chaotic days following the death of the general, when the high priest and his faithful decided to abandon the coalition and take full control by forming a new government. This new order forced their fundamental beliefs on you or simply, made you a noncitizen.

Arthur found himself rubbing his temples. He always felt he had let his people down. The people of the mountains had been betrayed and then banned from representing themselves in the new government because they were not of the faith. The representatives they did have down in the capital neither were from the mountains nor lived in the mountain region. Yet for whatever reason, the people of the mountains still looked to Arthur for leadership, and this often left him at odds with their so-called representatives and their government.

Arthur hoped to be able to stay out of this oncoming conflict, and that the remoteness and isolation of his village could again offer a buffer to insulate him and his young family against another looming crisis. Yet, if his aunt had been right about the feeling that sometimes woke him in the morning, he again might have some role to play. This morning may even have been a call to some greater action. For now, he would just have to wait, and if or when the time came to act, he would know and do just that.

That moment came sooner than Arthur expected when Mairwyn's voice startled him out of his thoughts. "Arthur? Are you up here?"

Arthur did not need to answer. Mairwyn had already rounded the corner of the stairway. "We have guests," she said in a slightly harsh tone.

When Arthur entered the inn's small lobby, Harmon walked over to greet him. Arthur noted that several men in high-ranking uniforms accompanied Harmon.

"Good to see you again, Arthur," said Harmon with a warm smile.

"So, to what do we owe the pleasure of your visit?" asked Arthur as Mairwyn came up beside him.

Harmon turned toward Mairwyn. "You look as beautiful as ever, Mairwyn, and let me assure you that I'm not here to arrest anyone. I am here in search of some much-needed advice from an old friend." Harmon turned to look at Arthur again. "That is if you can still accept me as one." After a brief pause, Harmon continued. "Can you at least hear an old friend out?"

"I always have time for an old friend," replied Arthur. "Can we take this into the inn's office?" Harmon gave a quick nod, and they started out of the lobby. The four officers began to follow, but Harmon waved them off and asked them to wait. Mairwyn veered off toward the kitchen as Arthur and Harmon stepped into the office.

"Your friends out there seem a bit uneasy," said Arthur as they sat down in the large chairs by the fireplace.

"This is gravely serious, Arthur, for those men out in your lobby and me. We are at a crossroads, one that will not only affect our lives but everyone who has been disowned and ostracized by my government. There are events that are rapidly spinning out of control down in the capital. So, if you haven't already heard, let me give you the quick details."

Harmon briefed Arthur on what had recently occurred, that a nonbeliever, who was shot and killed while trying to escape had assassinated the grand priest. Harmon told Arthur about the man known only as "the farmer" who seemed to be consolidating his position as the successor to the grand priest. He was doing this by firing up The Faithful, telling them that the only way to solve this problem once and for all was to make all nonbelievers convert. If they refused, they would become enemies of the state. If it was a war the heretics wanted, then a war to end all wars is what they would get.

"Arthur, I've met this man on a few occasions, and he scares me. He was a part of the grand priest's inner circle. How he got there, I'm not sure. I think he started out as a security advisor."

Mairwyn entered the office with coffee. "I've offered coffee to the officers in the lobby, but they politely declined. Would either one of you like some?" Both men nodded.

"Arthur, before I give you the farmer's ultimatum letter, I would like you to hear me out." Arthur nodded to Harmon as Mairwyn quietly sat down at the desk.

"Nine years ago, you told me that what the high priest was in the process of doing to the people of this country was wrong. I refused to listen to you. I rejected your warnings. I've since come to realize that you have been right about many things. That what you warned could happen, did happen. I was required to do things that did not make me proud, and I've seen things that have made me feel ashamed. Yet during that time, I felt powerless to change anything."

"Now, Arthur, I am at a point where I need to stand up for what is truly right. Those officers out there," he said as he pointed in the direction of the lobby, "share my feelings, and we are ready to stand against this farmer fellow. We already hold an area between the mountains and the capital. But we are less than a third of the total army, and of that, we are not even certain how many of our men will stand with us."

"Arthur, we come here to ask for more than your support. The people of the mountains must be prepared to defend themselves.

We need to stand together, or none of us will have any hope for a future." Harmon paused, and Arthur remained silent. "Or you will just accept the terms of the farmer." Harmon reached into his coat pocket and pulled out a letter along with a smallish tube. He handed the ultimatum letter to Arthur.

Arthur skimmed through the document. "You're going to need more than just the help of my people, Harmon," Arthur replied. "Much more help. You will need a new coalition."

"No, Arthur," replied Harmon. "*You* are going to need a new coalition. They will not trust or follow me. But they will follow you."

Harmon got up, but Arthur stayed seated and started to reread the letter. Harmon started fiddling with the tube in his hand and walked over to the fireplace.

"What's in the tube?" asked Mairwyn from the desk.

Harmon snorted. "It's a portrait of the farmer. He wants every family to hang it next to the portrait of the grand priest, which we all have hanging in our homes. I think I should like to burn it."

"Can I see it before you do?" asked Mairwyn.

"Sure," said Harmon, and he walked over and handed it to Mairwyn.

Mairwyn carefully opened one end of the tube and pulled the portrait out. After a long look, she broke the silence in the room. "You can tell a lot about a person by the look in their eyes. This farmer fellow, his eyes are cold and lifeless. It's as if he doesn't have a soul. How could a man like this come to replace your grand priest?"

Arthur shot up out of his chair and strode over to the desk. Mairwyn handed the picture to him. After a quick glance, he asked Mairwyn if Itanni was up yet.

"She's in the kitchen with Nelka. What is it, Arthur?" asked Mairwyn.

"Have her go and fetch Mathias from the brickyard and tell her to bring him to the inn's office as quickly as she can."

After what seemed like an hour, Mathias entered the room, breathing heavily from his fast walk. "I'm a seventy-one-year-old man; are you trying to have your sweet little nine-year-old girl kill me?"

Arthur offered Mathias one of the chairs in front of the desk. As soon as he was seated, Arthur handed him the picture.

Mathias shuddered. "You are trying to kill me. I don't need to see a picture of that monster. He already haunts my dreams."

"I don't understand, Arthur," said Harmon. "What is so important about the farmer's portrait?"

"That isn't a farmer—that is the field marshal, and he's nothing more than a cold-hearted murderer," said Mathias.

Arthur stood up and addressed the group, which now included the four officers who came in while they waited for Mathias. "I will join you in this, and with my support, I know that the people of the mountains will answer your call. I will also do what I can to try and rebuild the coalition, but..." Arthur said and paused before continuing. "We—each of us here—must understand that we cannot, can *never*, accept this ultimatum or fight against it on our own."

From out of the corner of his eye, Arthur could see Mairwyn openly weeping. "But I will ask one more important thing from each of you. That we all work to bring this man to justice." Arthur held up the portrait of the farmer. "He is not who he claims to be. He is a cold-hearted killer who is responsible for the torture and the murder of hundreds, possibly thousands of people during and after the protest marches against the king. So we, each of us, must make this fight a fight for truth and a fight for justice. Justice for all those lives he coldly and brutally destroyed."

"But I think to accomplish this; we need proof of the field marshal's crimes. We need to find the hard evidence—the mass graves that Mathias and I know to exist. To do that, I think we are going to have to find Mathias's old friend, the chief constable, or at least someone else Mathias might remember who worked in that precinct jail."

Arthur sat down, slouching heavily in his chair and looked at each person gathered in the room. "To be honest with all of you, I don't think we can win this fight, even if I can rebuild the coalition. If we cannot find the truth, if we cannot find credible evidence against the field marshal—the farmer—we are bound to fail."

"However, if we can somehow uncover it, and the proof is solid enough, then his supporters may start to splinter. If the people know the truth about this man, their support for him may even collapse right out from underneath him. If we can make that happen, then we have a chance, a good chance, of winning this fight."

"For the truth, then," stated Harmon.

"For justice," echoed the four officers.

"For the truth and justice...yes," answered Arthur. "However, each of you here needs to understand that from this point forward, we must stand above our enemy. We must be guided by the highest levels of our integrity and steered by wisdom, for if we do not stand by these two principles, then the people of this country will not trust us or be willing to support us."

Section 7

Of Liberty and Freedom

Freedom without equality, respect, and justice is anarchy. Therefore, freedom can never be free, for in this lawlessness comes disparity, intimidation, and depravity. In this, we lose the enlightened side of our humanity. Instead, we earn our liberty through the principles of equality, respect, and justice. So again, freedom can never be free, for in striving for everyone's liberty, we earn our own freedoms. These principles define our humanity for our greater good. This is what truly sets us apart and allows us to live freely.

God, Leadership, and Government

The concept of government is strictly a human endeavor and is not directly relevant to God. That is because only the individual, not the establishment, has a direct connection to God. What is important is how we manage ourselves within the social organizations we have created. At the individual level, our spiritual foundation puts God and peace first. Our mandates after this are to recognize that every person's life is sacred and that, no matter the color of our skin or our sex, we are all equal.

These two mandates need to become the foundation of our societies, religions, and even governments. So how can we ensure that our institutions meet or continue to meet these two mandates? First, we need to remember that we have leadership and governments because it is the will and the need of the people to have them.

From the very beginnings of human society, we have looked to our elders to ensure the survival and success of our families or tribes. As humanity became more successful and competition for resources grew, our need for order, stability, and security strengthened that necessity for leadership. However, human beings have a unique duality that is both earthly and spiritual. These natures impart two different characteristics of leadership.

Our older, animalistic nature puts the strongest at the top of the pecking order for as long as this alpha can maintain it. Our spiritual nature not only heightens our situational awareness, but it also augments our problem-solving skills and our adaptability. Herein lies the root conflict within leadership—to what degree a leader's characteristics are earthly, animalistic strength and power versus spiritual, inspired insight and intellect. It is in this second one which has the power to broadens our understanding of each other, our world, and ourselves. When a leader embraces the spiritual side of leadership, he or she gains the wisdom that not only makes those around this alpha successful but also gives each generation associated with their stewardship the knowledge of how to be successful.

Another real problem with leadership is how it is passed on. Even in ancient times, those people knew the critical importance and value of a smooth transition to a new leader within their group. A good changeover minimized any disruption of daily life and helped maintain harmony. Poor shifts in power can create conflict that divides and weakens the group. In the worst scenarios, it is highlighted by assassinations and the slaughter of the innocent.

More problematic still is a move to an heir or the next-strongest contender. This simply does not always guarantee a good leader. This is especially true if a leader is chosen by consensus but has built-in biases against certain individuals within the group. The same could be said if the group has divided loyalties to different candidates. Fortunately or unfortunately, natural leaders tend to rise to the top, just as they also have a tendency to attract followers. That being said, strength and wisdom are not always going to be found together or even be in balance within each leader.

Poor leadership often relies on a core following with absolute loyalty to ensure the continuation of their power, regardless of the cost. Good leaders will distinguish themselves by understanding and making the most of both sides of these earthly and spiritual natures. They will actively play a role in choosing and training their successors. Ideally, these choices are made not solely from their heirs but rather from individuals within the community with the highest potential and ability to lead.

Some leaders will understand the importance of maintaining a level of integrity, equality, and respect, not just for those in their own group but for everyone. These leaders recognize the importance and the sanctity of the individual and work to apply these principals to our greater humanity. The best kind of leader does not demand respect but rather earns it through integrity and wisdom. Respect that is just commanded and not returned quickly crumbles. This is especially true when crises arise. Yet almost anything can be accomplished by the leader who has proven his or her worth and earned a measure of trust and admiration from all.

With our animalistic nature comes the need to fulfill our basic earthly necessities and desires, and with successful leadership come the prestige, privilege, and affluence to provide effortless fulfillment of those needs and wants. Long-term access to this lifestyle creates a deep-seated need to hold onto that position of authority and power regardless of the cost paid by the rest of humanity. History has proven that once leadership is established, it, for the most part, falls into lines of hereditary rulers.

Our earthly nature can have the most devastating effect on leadership, even with the best of leaders. The longer those who lead or the individuals supporting those leaders are in those positions of power, the less likely they are to let go of it. The harder they cling to that authority, the more determined they become to keep it. In the end, the two principles of the simplest of truths, equality and the sanctity of life, became the first casualties.

In times of peace and prosperity, hereditary leaders often govern with little thought given to anything different. This can even be reflected by the people themselves. The court or the central government surrounding the monarch rose up from the loyalty or subjugation of the people. The court's function was not only there to support their sovereign but also to ensure success by helping to manage the affairs of state. To a lesser extent, the court helps to facilitate the smooth ascension of an heir. In times of war and chaos, warriors can rise to prominence. These warlords can not only root out the worst and most ineffective of these hereditary rulers but also destroy some of the better ones.

Then again, human nature plays its part, and this typically leads to new lines of hereditary rulers, bringing with them the same underlying forms of corruption. In times of famine or great social strife, the people often reach out to their religious leaders for answers. This can propel those religious figures into seats of power. But this too can involve a level of corruption if these religious leaders simply become the foundation to another line of hereditary rulers.

Religious organizations are not immune to the corrupting effects of power, because even these groups can and will overlook the principles of the simplest of truths when it is problematic, inconvenient, or even a threat to the sustainment of their rule over their faithful. This pertains even more so to minorities who are outside the mainstream faith, regardless of whether they are under any direct control or not.

This is why we must guarantee that the two principles of the simplest of truths become the foundation of our social, religious, and governmental institutions. This is why we cannot make any king, general, or priest infallible or absolute because they are not; they are all human. As humans, we all encompass the same dual natures that, no matter how hard we try, can never be separated. No one person, army, or religious institution can rule with complete power without eventually falling into corruption. The longer an individual or people embedded in that system of rule retain those seats of authority, the higher the threat of corruption. The consolidation of prestige, privileges, and affluence can often lead to a self-proclaimed or implied God-given right to rule over the people.

In the beginning, it was the need of the people who put the strongest and the wisest leaders in their roles. The people's support of their leaders became the foundation for the concept of what is, government. This ancient arrangement was originally based on trust, and this trust still needs to run both ways. It is a relationship, and as such, it is kept healthy by a conversation, a dialogue of discovery. In the past, the elders would pass on their knowledge and worldly wisdom to the younger generation, while the youth with their strength helped to provide the basics needed for everyone to survive in an often unforgiving land.

Apart from this more intimate family or tribal leadership setting, our greatest threat comes when the will of the people is overshadowed or replaced with the needs of our leaders. This includes those individuals who run those governmental institutions that support those leaders. When those who have been commissioned to serve and protect put their own self-serving interests ahead of the people, it only leads to corruption. In some cases, it can lead to certain groups of people being viewed as worthless. When people have no perceived worth, their freedom and livelihood can easily be stifled, and their potential is stripped from them. This can lead to the worst possible forms of oppression, where the sanctity of life is merely forfeit. This is especially true if a person or group of people is viewed as inconvenient, problematic, or a threat to the continuation of that government, religious group, or its leadership.

When the rights of citizens are denied by the government that has sworn to protect them, it is the beginning of the end for equality, respect, and liberty. When any government takes up arms against its own people, it is the starting point of a downward spiral into chaos, destruction, and death. If the sustainment of any government or its leadership is contingent on the repression and coercion of its people, the consequences can be far-reaching. These events can often eclipse the borders of any country and may ultimately have a catastrophic effect on all of humanity.

When we lose sight of the two mandates of the simplest of truths that of equality and the sanctity of life, we no longer have peace or even God in our hearts. By ignoring these truths, we have defied God. We have never been given a license to kill or to kill in the name of God. Yet it has been proclaimed as such, repeatedly throughout history, for nothing more than our own self-serving ends.

The Ring Governing

The basic principles of government in our modern world are generally broken down into a spectrum of ideologies fixed between two wide-ranging and often contrasting philosophies. You could say conservative versus liberal, capitalism versus communism, or even religious versus secular. Collectively, these only reflect an exclusive or an inclusive viewpoint of different ideologies and each extreme can be categorized as either narrow or broad in its scope.

The problem with the first, narrow-minded, or more traditional of these two ideologies of scope is that it encourages an egocentric lifestyle for those who have success and power. This often comes at the expense or labor of others, with no real sense of respect or remorse for the exploited. The successful few, feel justified in their actions and believe they have earned everything they have gained. That these successful few have every right to those profits, regardless of how they acquired them. The general community becomes nothing more than a marginalized society that lives just slightly above subsistence.

The problem with the second, broad-minded, or more radical of the two ideologies of scope is that it is short on incentives for the individual to be successful. The one thing that matters is that the collective whole is productive. The individual cannot aspire to be more prosperous than his or her neighbor. When there is no inspiration to do greater things in life, there is no motivation to go above and beyond what is absolutely necessary to survive. Again, the general community becomes nothing more than a marginalized society that lives just slightly above subsistence.

When looking at these opposing philosophies of scope, we need to understand that there are two other equally powerful factors influencing those lines of scope. The best way to explain the dynamics of these other opposing concepts is that it represents a line of control that runs perpendicular to the line of scope. On one side is reserved authority, which attempts to balance governmental power with individual freedom. On the other is an absolute authority with the suppression of free will. Here the will of the people is repressed, and the will of the government or religious state becomes supreme, all-encompassing, and uncompromising. The two opposing forces pull on that horizontal line of scope, broadening and bending it from a single line into a ring. Just as the earth is not flat, these ideologies are not actually linear to each other; instead, they are opposing philosophies of scope and control that reside on opposite sides and at different points around a circle.

At the top of this ring is the balanced approach of a measured democracy. This type of government embraces equality, respect, and justice without compromising individual liberty or free will. It assures the people freedom and fundamental human rights. It should symbolize equal representation for all, through freely elected citizens serving in their government with integrity and wisdom. This measured democracy should strive to protect individual liberty and allow its people to work toward their fullest potential. This type of government relies on checks and balances of power and adopts a dialogue of truth and discovery through robust ethics codes and unbiased enforcement of those codes. It also allows for full accountability and unobstructed oversight by the people over their government to help maintain the integrity and quality of that government.

On the bottom side of this ring of governing are the tyrannical regimes or dictatorships. These often highlight the subjugation and repression of the people through intimidation, disparity, and depravity. This style of government relies on fear as a way to preserve its complete and exploitive power over the lives of its people and can include the brutal suppression of any opposition.

This type of government will stop at nothing to maintain power. The individual's free will and their human rights are often ignored. The reality here is that there is no respect, sensitivity, or remorse by the government for the suffering of its people. The only thing that is important is the state and those who wield power within that state. Repeatedly throughout history, these regimes have grown their roots through both very narrow-minded conservative ideologies or extremely liberal ones. Those within these governments can easily be corrupted by the influence of the power of authority or even by a perceived God-given right.

Within this ring of governing, true north is represented by the measured democracy, which enhances our humanity. The key word here is measured, which should be defined first as "restrained," followed by "stately" and "dignified." As the measure of a person is defined by integrity and wisdom, the measure of a government should be defined by the integrity and the wisdom of those people serving within it.

What we really need to understand is that the farther we move from true north, either to the left or to the right, the more universally generic or closed-minded governments, or societies become. The more extreme the shift to one side or the other, the more it affects our individual rights and free will. If we are not careful, these big swings to either the left or the right can tip the balance against the people and open the door for an oppressive regime or a dictatorship.

When political change sweeps through a country, those movements drive change for better or worse. The groups forcing the change often start by defining and describing themselves as exactly what the people are looking for in a government. Yet when any measure of control is stripped away from the people on either side of the conflict, it can degrade into the oppression of an uncompromising regime.

When we look closely at what lies beneath the picture painted by any group or government, the truth cannot be hidden. With the absence of the people's fundamental human rights, the truth is undeniable. With the absence of the people's liberty and the freedom to express themselves, the truth is indisputable. With a deficiency of integrity and wisdom, the truth is irrefutable. With the lack of respect, honesty, and justice, the truth is incontestable. Ignoring the mandates of the simplest of truths— that of equality and respect for the sanctity of life—the truth is unquestionable. When any group or government denies any of these principles, these mandates, it can be placed in the ring of governing where it honestly belongs—at the bottom.

The Measured Democracy

The way to prevent a government and its leaders from becoming corrupted by power, prestige, privileges, and affluence are through the checks and balances of the measured democracy. This type of government is always administered by its freely elected citizens serving their local communities and their country. Foremost, there must be an equal representation to ensure each regional, religious, and ethnic group is treated fairly within that government. The people should also have a public voice and the freedom to express themselves. There should also be an unobstructed oversight by the people in regards to their government and unbiased enforcement of ethics so that those elected citizens serve with integrity and with wisdom.

The single most crucial article after this is not allowing these elected citizens to make a lifelong career within that government. We need to make sure that at every level of government, from our city leaders to our national leaders, no one should serve in those elected or appointed positions of authority for an extended period.

We must also reduce the level of influence businesses, religious groups, and special-interest organizations have on our government. Here too there must be checks and balances that prevent the privileged and the affluence from creating policies and laws that are one-sided or too narrowly focused on a particular group's agenda. We must also limit the level of influence these groups have on the election process. Left unchecked, this can interfere with the core principles of a measured democracy—ensuring equal representation for all, defending our fundamental human rights, safeguarding the sanctity of life and protecting our environment for the generations to come.

The will of the people provides the authority for a government to govern. Given that authority, that government should provide stability, security, and a united voice for their entire country. The people's trust in their government should never be compromised, not by the government itself or by special-interest groups. It becomes the responsibility for everyone to ensure that no group, within or outside the government, imparts any self-serving ideologies and that those groups are not allowed to chart a course for the nation at the expense of the people or that negatively affects the quality of life of the people.

A true measured democracy also needs to have a population empowered by knowledge. The government of any high-quality democratic republic provides opportunities for all their citizens through education for all and the freedom of the individual to pursue their fullest potential. Not only does this provide the basis for a strong economy, but it also has the added benefit of creating a population with the capacity for any citizen to seek an elected office, not to mention a society capable of asking the right questions of those candidates running for elected offices.

The measured democracy is our best hope for ensuring that the mandates of the simplest of truths are incorporated into the core of our governments. At the same time, the measured democracy has the added ability to minimize the risk of corruption.

Therefore, the footings to a sustainable, measured democracy should be set in the two mandates that guarantee equality and sanctity of life for everyone. The foundation should be laid within an educated society with a commitment to continue educating the masses. This allows the fullest realization of the people's potential and the largest pool of citizens with the greatest ability to lead. The walls of our civil institutions are raised by those freely elected citizens serving with wisdom and integrity in their local, state, and national governments. Our roof, our protection from the corrupting elements, are covered through term limits, restricting the influence of narrowly focused interest groups, businesses, and religious organizations. It also should include oversight of the government by the people and unbiased enforcement of ethics.

This is the way it has to be, because no king, general, priest, or their supporting governments can rule with absolute authority without becoming corrupted by the powers of prestige, privilege, and affluence.

Walking Out of the Dark: Part Seven

Our Inherent Essence

Beginnings.
Life, a spark of energy wakes, an apparition that moves like the wind jumping from boulder to boulder as it bounds along the spine of the earth, sending shivers spinning and rolling in all directions.

Heart of earth.
Love, the sentient soil breathes life into all that touches its heart, sown with deep thoughtfulness it embarrasses the old and infuses the new with purpose, a living essence that transcends time and generations.

Spirits in the temple forest.
Mindfulness, light and dark at play cause soft shadows to perpetually shift under the boughs of the ancient trees, the great sentinels watch as day and night turns in a continuous dance, as restless shapes endlessly move about the forest.

Breath upon the grassland.
Truth, the land sighs, and the restless wind meanders as a cold ether descends on the prairie, the air's demur as sharp as the hardest stones that lie underfoot, an unseen force defined only by its effect upon the swaying grass.

Legacy of the mountains.
Hope, the parhelion's pale eyes hold the sun as the frozen world pauses, all listen for a time when the roar of icy waters again tumbles down the mountains to fill the silver veins that refresh the land, a promise undimmed in the weak sunlight.

Ancient voices of the sky.
Respect, dark clouds gather on the horizon, lightning reveals ghostly faces in the billows that reach the very top of the sky, rolling thunder echoes their deep haunting voices and sends it rumbling down deep into life's core.

Soul of the earth.
Peace, the rain whispers softly, the spirit blurs as it falls down to seeps deep into slumber upon the bedrock, the living earth embraces the gift and gives it rest even as it is transformed to create life renewed.

Deep well of still water.
Integrity, a spark of energy wakes, a sprite springs forth bubbling and trickling to form a pool of long-forgotten wisdom, a clear clarity gained through the time spent in meditation within the deep inner stillness.

It had been three long years. Arthur was bone tired. He felt much older than his forty-eight years. He had worked tirelessly, most of the time from behind the scenes, keeping the coalition together and shoring it back up when issues arose—and there were always issues. Early on, he had spent weeks and even months at a time away from his family as the war dragged on.

Through that time, Harmon and Elias become his greatest allies. They had gone to great lengths to mask Arthur's actual role and protect his identity from all but the most important people. Arthur understood his critical role and the reason behind their need for security and secrecy. Lately, that arrangement had become a necessity, but it was one that also allowed him to be at home more often, though this left him cut off from regular communications.

Arthur had realized early on that this war was shaping up to be far worse than the previous two combined. Arthur saw it in the faces of the people he met during his travels. In those faces, Arthur could see fear, anger, and hate. This war had gone beyond cruel and brutal and was sparing no one from its savagery. This was what weighed heaviest on his mind.

Recently, the coalition had been able to track down the chief constable who had spared Mathias's and Arthur's lives, but he would not agree to help. That is until Mathias went to see him personally. Even then, he would not leave the remote lighthouse, which he operated and maintained. Nevertheless, he proved to be a wealth of knowledge about the time leading up to the fall of the last king.

Arthur had been home at his inn, which was currently being used as a hospital, for almost two months. This morning, Arthur received a brief message from Elias stating that much progress had been made, and a full report was to follow. Arthur had anxiously waited all day for more news. When no word had arrived by late afternoon, he retreated to the roof to watch the sun go down.

The sound of footsteps on the stairs roused Arthur from a light sleep. "Dad, are you up here?" It was Kaisa.

"Yes, sweetheart," replied Arthur.

"You have company. Oh, and I guess here he is right now."

Elias rounded the corner of the stairway. "Sir," he said and gave a quick bow.

"What's that all about?" said Arthur. "And don't call me sir. You know my name, and don't ever do that bowing thing to me again."

"Hmm, a bit testy tonight, aren't you?" Elias said teasingly.

"No...yes...never mind," replied Arthur. "I really hope you have some good news for a change. I sure could use it."

"In fact, I do. I have some good news, and I have some even greater news...and then I have some not-so-good news," said Elias. "I can give a full debriefing, but might I suggest we find a more comfortable place to talk? The air up here is getting a bit cool for my liking."

Arthur and Elias retired to the kitchen. The inn's office had been given over to the hospital and was used primarily by Dr. Mairwyn and her staff. Arthur set a kettle of water on to boil and sat down. After talking and catching up on each other's families, Elias finally started his report.

"The good news is that the old chief constable came through for us. Not only did he give us directions to those mass graves you and Mathias knew existed somewhere, but he also provided many of the names from the Royal Guard unit that served under the field marshal at the time of the protest-march massacre."

"From there, Harmon and I worked in different directions. I was sent looking for those mass graves, and Harmon went looking for old military records. So far, we have located two mass gravesites. Each must contain hundreds of remains, if not more."

"Harmon, however, had even more luck. He found some of the field marshal's original military records. We now know his real name, and we know his past. Harmon also found the records of about a dozen of the field marshal's royal guards, two of whom are still directly serving the field marshal, a.k.a. the farmer."

While Arthur was listening, the water had come to a boil. Arthur got up and set the tea to steep. After a few minutes, he grabbed two cups from the nearby cupboard. "Tea?" he asked. When Elias nodded, he poured two cups and sat down again.

Elias took a sip of the hot tea and then continued. "From there, Harmon, with the help of the coalition, tracked down and arrested four of the old royal guards. When questioned, one confessed that he and a group of ex-royal guards had fired the first shots that started the general's massacre of The Faithful, which we know started the second war. According to this man, the field marshal planned to start another war. This man also said that, at the time, most of the few remaining members of the old royal guard had a deep hatred for the general but none more so than the field marshal himself. When we further questioned the others again, they all confirmed the first man's story."

"Arthur, when you first said that this war must be fought for the truth, I don't think very many of us took that to heart. Now, with all this evidence starting to roll in against the field marshal, I think it hit Harmon the hardest. He has taken this way too personally. A while back, he sent a message across the lines to someone he thought might honestly listen to him. He then took a huge risk and crossed over into the capital to present the evidence against the farmer in person."

Elias took another sip of tea then continued his narrative. "I'm not sure how he did it, but he got someone within The Faithful to listen. He is either the bravest man I know or the biggest fool. Anyway, from the last report that I have received from Harmon, The Faithful secretly arrested the two ex-royal guards that have been serving the farmer. They told each of them that the other had implicated them as the real murderer of the grand priest. Both denied the charges and then confessed that the farmer had actually done the killing himself."

"So now," continued Elias, "the whole thing *is* crumbling in on the farmer. The leadership within The Faithful seems to be struggling with how to deal with this betrayal from within their own inner circle. Unfortunately, this now leaves Harmon stuck inside the capital. He may even be in serious danger."

Elias took another sip of tea. "This is excellent tea."

"It is the mildest and smoothest tea I can find," said Arthur. "Mairwyn won't let me have anything too strong, or it'll keep me up at night."

Elias chuckled softly, but after a sideways glance at Arthur, he cleared his throat and quickly moved on with his report. "Now it seems we have another problem—the coalition is feuding again. Some of the members want to start an all-out offensive to take the capital, while the leadership within The Faithful is still reeling. Harmon's men are threatening to abandon the coalitions if any attacks are carried out against the capital before Harmon is safely out of there. The only thing that I can say for certain is that the coalition will not act until after they have heard from you."

Arthur blew on the hot liquid and then looked Elias directly in the eyes. "The way I see it," he said, "Harmon has gained the ear of someone he can trust, someone of a high enough rank to keep him safe. Most likely, it is a member of the inner circle. He also must have someone he can trust for getting his information out of the capital."

"So we need to do two things straight away," continued Arthur. "The coalition needs to agree on an immediate cease-fire and a temporary truce. What the coalition needs to understand is that the worst possible action they can take right now is to attack the capital. Not just for Harmon's safety but also for this country's future."

"Second," Arthur continued. "We need to get a message back to Harmon, and since he has someone he trusts to get information out, then we have a way to get our information back into him."

"But we don't have any way to send for that messenger," protested Elias. "And what if Harmon doesn't or can't send any more messages? How are we going to get your message through to him?"

"Harmon will send him out again," replied Arthur.

"How do you know that, Arthur? How is he supposed to know what we need him to do?"

"When the coalition openly calls for a cease-fire and a temporary truce, whoever is protecting Harmon will share that information with him, and Harmon *will* send out the messenger again." Arthur paused before continuing. "When that messenger arrives, they must take my note back to Harmon."

"So what is the plan, then?" asked Elias.

The Simplest of Truths

"I will address and hopefully persuade the coalition that the best option right now is to sit down and talk peace with The Faithful. Harmon will need to convince his contact within The Faithful to meet with us to negotiate a peace plan. I hope that Harmon and his benefactor can weed out the worst of the farmer's followers and then put together a group that they can safely bring to the peace talks. Hopefully, too, they will be the type of people who might just be willing to listen."

"There are a lot of *ifs* here, Arthur," said Elias. "So where do you think this meeting can take place without causing all kinds of suspicion?"

After a long pause and much thought, Arthur continued. "We will meet on the twenty-third of this month, in the Grand Hall at the old royal summer palace," replied Arthur.

"But that is only weeks away!" cried Elias.

"So, you, Harmon, and the coalition are going to have to act quickly. We have to act now, without delay, if we want to take full advantage of this opportunity for peace."

"Yes, sir...I mean, we will not let you down, Arthur," replied Elias.

* * *

As the war-hardened men and women gathered and took their seats in the Grand Hall of a long-dead king, Arthur stood and bowed. It was the signal for a small army of nurses to enter the large hall. Each nurse carried a newborn infant swaddled in similar blankets. Each person gathered there was asked to hold and cradle one of the infants.

At this point, Arthur addressed the assembly. "You asked me why I have asked you to be here today, and I will answer you shortly, but let me first ask a few more things of you. Look, just look at the infant you hold, and tell me: Is it a boy or a girl? Is this child of your faith, of your culture, or not? What does their future hold? What will become of this child?" To this, there was only silence. Arthur continued. "We are here for these infants, the most vulnerable, and helpless among us. They are counting on *us* for their future. Yet they are *our* future. So I ask you, what kind of a future are *we* going to give them?" After a long pause, Arthur continued.

"We simply cannot keep moving down the road we are currently traveling. How many more lives will be cut short, and how many more families will be destroyed?" Arthur swept his arm in the direction of the nearest baby. "How many more innocent souls will be crushed by the brutality of hate that is committed countless times every day before we realize the error of our ways, destroying ourselves and our future in the process?" He paused again. "Peace must start somewhere. It needs to start here. It must start with each and every one of you."

"It is up to each of you to come to terms with each other and then find a way to peacefully move forward. We must endeavor to move forward and forge a new government, one that affords equality for all protects the life and livelihood of each individual and allows those people to realize their fullest potential. If you cannot do this for the person across from you, then do it for the little life you are holding now." Arthur waited to let the weight of his words sink in and then he nodded at the nurse closest to him. All the infants were scooped up by the nurses and swept out of the Great Hall, back to the arms of their waiting mothers.

Arthur continued addressing the gathering. "The unwinding of this country happened when its people became so polarized and embedded in their own ideologies that they could not and would not accept compromise, let alone sense the dangers that were just beyond the scope of their narrow vision. Our divisive cultures and politics created an environment that weakened our country to the point where it crumbled in on itself. Not just once but three times. Three wars we have fought against each other." Arthur paused. "We need to re-forge the rusted and broken sword of our republic. It will be hard work, and there will be sweat on our brows, but with the right amount of heat and with every blow of the hammer, the blade will grow stronger."

"This new sword of our republic needs to be forged through equality, shaped and strengthened on the anvil of truth with the hammer of justice, tempered in the cooling waters of peace, and sharpened to a razor's edge on the stone of integrity." Arthur paused again. "Without equality, the blade will remain impure. Without truth and justice, the blade will be twisted and weak. Without peace, the blade will be brittle and break. Without the sharpness of its integrity, this sword will never succeed in the job it was crafted for, or be used as it was intended. The strength of that blade is not to create war, but rather to guard and preserve peace, equality and the sanctity of life from those who would squash them."

After another pause, Arthur continued again. "We are all citizens. We are the stewards of this country. We are the swords. Without equality, we are tainted and immoral. Without truth and justice, we are corruptible. Without peace, we are weak and easily divided. Without integrity and wisdom, we will never succeed in doing the job our people need, want, and expect us to do. The task before us is to create a government that is honest and fair to all of its citizens, regardless of their ethnic or religious background."

"What we do here will set the tone for tomorrow. However, it will be for nothing if we, each of us, do not do our part to influence those who look to us for leadership. To show the people, by our honest dedication, the importance of the work we as a united federation are striving to create. The examples we set here will go the farthest to calm the fear, the anger, and the hate of *our* people. It will be through our own effort and the continued support we show within our own communities, that we will build a new trust and faith between all of *our* people, for this new government we are working to forge. It is my hope that one day we can accept each other not just as equals but as neighbors and friends once again."

Arthur remained standing, and the gathering remained quiet. After a long pause and a glance at almost everyone in that Grand

Hall, he broke the silence again. "So, who of you within this assembly is ready to fully embrace the tasks and challenges we have ahead of us?"

Although there was an undercurrent of murmuring, many sideways glances, and guarded expressions, everyone eventually called out their names.

"Then let's start building the foundation to our future," said Arthur. "One brick at a time and one row upon the last."

FIN

Section 8

Currents of Thought

We so often build walls around our emotions and ourselves as a defense. Whether you keep the wall up or tear it down is a choice you make based on what your heart is telling you. Moreover, the heart can sometimes be wrong, but this is only our inner wisdom based on your own experiences. One good choice, at times, cannot be made without making a few bad ones and sometimes choices cannot be labeled good or bad until after you have lived them. You will not always make wise decisions, but you can gain wisdom from the choices you have lived through. All anyone can do is square up our shoulders and level our eyes on the road ahead, to continue moving forward, fortified in the knowledge that God's peace is always close, and that, regardless of the choices we have to make along the way, we are strong enough to handle the outcome.

Circles of Life

If you think about it, our mind and our emotions are extensions of the spirit as much as our body is an extension of the world we live in. We are the point of connection between these two. Yet, life is about relationships, all of the possible connections; it starts in the family, and for better or worse, we are reliant on our social families as much as our ecological interactions. We exist at the point where all four of these factors overlap. We are bound to the worldly. We are and will always be, mutually dependent on and mutually supportive of our social and ecological circles. We have also been elevated and enlightened by the spirit.

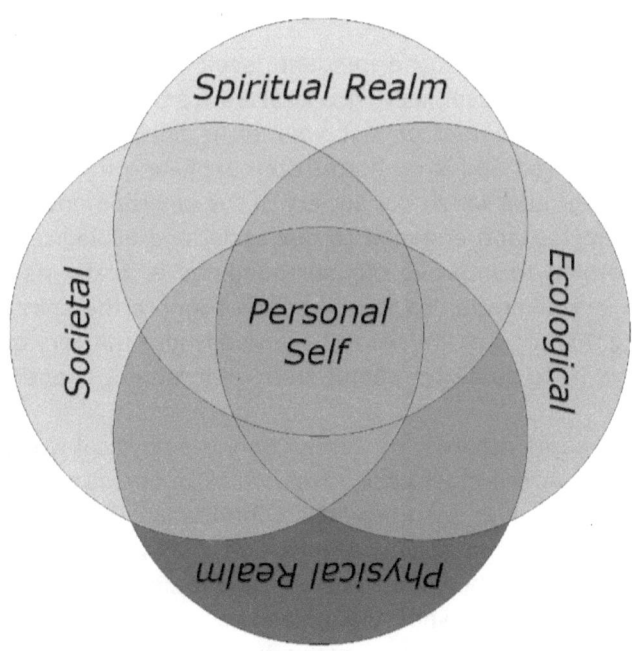

Putting aside humankind's worst flaws, we can still consider ourselves a success story. Maybe this is because we have been guided by a divine, inner strength, a blessed people who have been given the tools to overcome our shortcomings. Our long-term and continuing success, however, will require us to reach a little deeper into ourselves. Each of us needs to learn how to balance and live in harmony with all four circles of life. We, the total sum of humanity are quickly reaching a point that, without this measured approach to living, our future, our way of life will not be sustainable.

For us, it is critical that we include our relationship with the environment in the core of a holistic approach to living. Because, all four of these circles of life influence and are interconnected to one another, and each needs nurturing, in its own way, to keep our whole system healthy. Without a caring attitude towards our social and ecological environments, a healthy, balanced lifestyle is not obtainable, and the mind and the body will never truly be in harmony. When our environment suffers, we suffer. When our society is in chaos, so are our lives.

We also cannot closed-mindedly seek to improve ourselves spiritually while disconnecting ourselves from our social circles. Seeking enlightenment of just yourself is another form of selfishness or greed and is no better than exploiting the of the most vulnerable groups within our society or the environment. We must stay connected and engaged to our social and ecological circles, to do nothing to improve our surroundings is nearly as bad as causing it to degrade. So too, we cannot ignore the spirit; for in rejecting this circle of life, we will eventually lose the very qualities that allow us to be better people from generation to generation.

In the same regards, we cannot defy the physical world's natural course. At the most basic level, we have one straightforward role in life, which is ensuring life's continuation. This has less to do with how human society thinks and works on a day-to-day basis but rather, in how it approaches and maintains a productive, mutually supportive, and sustainable population over time. The winners here will not be the ones with alternative ideas about our essential role. Rather, real success will come to those who made an effort and invested their time to give life and a sense of purpose to the children who will inherit tomorrow. It is through those children, the ones who will come to understand this essential role and continue those promises of life, that will shape the future.

Outside of our physical realities, our life-long vision should be to leave nature and our society in a better state than when we entered it. For each of us, this starts by accepting the peace within, the God within or maybe just the idea of a connection to a higher conscious and living universe. This spirals outwards from each of us when we embrace the mandates of equality and the sanctity of life. These truths should become the bedrock of our lives. Building upon this, we also need to adopt the principles of respect, honesty, integrity, and wisdom. These values are the living soil that rests upon the bedrock of the simplest of truths and out of this fertile soil thrives truth and love.

Regardless of a person's social, religious, or ethnic background, if we all can embrace these truths and principles as our foundation, then it does not matter what we, others, or different societies choose to build on top of it, so long as we all stay true to that simple but common groundwork. We must also take this one step farther and apply these principles and that same measured approach to that relationship which we all share with our environment. If we can do this, we can then create a better state of being for ourselves, our societies, the world we share and ultimately, the world our grandchildren will share. I hope that, at the very least, even if it is in the smallest of ways, we might inspire each other to improve our earthly, human, and spiritual ecology.

A Glance Back

I did not start this project with the idea that it would become a book. I wrote the first short, "I Am Who Am," in early 2002 after a rather slow commute to work where I had a lot of time to reflect on an idea. A second short, "Eye of the Hurricane," followed sometime later. It came out of one line I had written in the earlier work. Even later, I added what is now called "The Peace Within," but unlike most of the individual essays in this book, that one has gone through a long series of changes. At the time, I was not looking to do anything with these three short stories. I was just putting my thoughts into words.

In 2009, I started writing again, expanding, and following a similar line of reasoning. I started with the "Four Cores" and then "Between the Two," followed by "The Simplest of Truths," "Mass Transit," "Whitewash," and "Traffic." These five essays and one parable were written in a relatively short period. Those five along with the earlier three stories became the framework of what I believe is life's simplest of truths.

"The King, the General, and the Priest" and "God, Leadership, and Government" followed about six months later, the latter of which was later expanded then divided into three parts. After a break of about, a year came "Both Sides of the Coin," and a couple of months after that I wrote "The Conversation." Within the next six months came a longer piece, which eventually became "Our Legacy," "The Promise," and "Building Tomorrow."

With the story "Walking out of the Dark," I wanted to expand and bring some life to a couple of the earlier parables. This was when I thought that I might have enough for a book if I could find a way to blend it all together. To do this, I intertwined the story with the essays and parables.

Two of the poems included in the book are those I had written about thirty years ago, but the rest is new. Most of the transitional pieces and the more recent poems were written in the summer and fall of 2013 as a way to bring some additional structure to the whole manuscript. I worked on the graphics between 2011 and 2014 because I felt some visuals were needed to go along with some of the concepts. Two of these became the front and back cover art. Later, I added the poem "Winter's Renewing Spirit" to the beginning of "Walking out of the Dark: Part Four". I also added the chapter "Circles of Life" along with the accompanying artwork.

In this 2nd Edition, I added three new chapters (Section 3) and other content. In that process, I reordered some of the chapters and arranged them into sections to make them easier to navigate.

The objective of this book eventually became twofold. First, I wanted to build an awareness that might allow you to create the right environment within yourself and from there, this might help you define, and find the better path at every crossroads in life. Moving forward this might help you make positive changes in your life and in your world. Second, I wanted to remind everyone to always consider the effects of your actions and, if needed, be accountable for the repercussions, because any choice or decision you make on your own path through life can become a defining point for you or someone else's life-changing event.

Clarify and Define

For me, when I first published this book in 2015, it put me on a course I am not always overly comfortable with, and I may never completely be. So, at times, I find that I need to continue to clarify and define my viewpoint. I believe, first and foremost and without question, in God. Call it the Conscious Living Universe, Peace, or God. It's all the same to me, and I do not say this to refute anyone's beliefs, and my intent is not to offend people. But, there is more to the Universe, to Peace or even God, then just believing or just existence.

What is the Universe or Peace or God without the relationship? What are we without our relationships? What are our relationships or even Love worth without honesty, integrity, wisdom, or even forgiveness? I grew up with the expectation that I should always try to love my neighbor, to treat others the way you want to be treated, and these should be the ideals we should strive to live by. Yet, what is love without equality, what is love without nurturing and guidance? What is love without guarding and protecting each other's life? These simple truths have become the foundation for me, and they are the heart of my book. When each person is given the right foundation; it then honestly does not matter what they or we choose to build on top of it, so long as we all stay true to that simple but common groundwork.

Earlier in the book, I asked this question. What do you think is essential to God in regards to humanity? That we continue to persecute those we believe are immoral because they do not live up to what we feel is God's moral standard. Or, do you think it is more important to God that we learn not to discriminate against those individuals despite what we may deem as immoral? If you are one who will not be moved in your attitude, then I hope God has mercy on your soul, to forgive that debt you gain through the merciless cruelty you committed on the ones you discriminated against or persecuted. So, let me repeat this. Every debt that we create and do not seek forgiveness for in our lifetime will be paid in full during our final judgment. Because it is as essential to forgive as it is to be forgiven, every debt we fail to forgive in our lifetime will also be held against us in our final judgment.

There is a fine line between honestly trying to help those lost souls, to unconsciously oppressing those who you feel have stayed and then mistreating the ones you believe are immoral. Regardless of how we feel about someone's lifestyle or culture, we are not entitled to disrespect them simply because they do not conform to our principles. Righteous indication does not justify hurtful and hateful actions. Remember, the Romans persecuted the Christian for much the same reasons. Just as the Christian's discriminated against and persecuted the Jews of Europe for centuries and Muslim's persecute those they view as infidels or allege to have committed blasphemy. Who is the one really being offended here, God? Maybe it is just you who is incensed?

When will our heartless persecution of those who are different for us, end? So again I ask, what do you think is important to God? We are not meant to judge those who are of a different faith, have different values, live different lifestyles, or who are just different from us. This is not a part of how God's intends us to live. We are also not being required to agree with or accept them but to merely acknowledge and respect them for who they are and let them live in peace just as they too should allow us to live in peace.

Looking behind this to the broader, worldly view, I do not think our different faiths necessarily need fundamental changes, they are still relevant, but our attitudes, our understanding, and our tolerance for those who are different from us or our own faith definitely requires soul-searching. It is on that individual level that this refocusing needs to be done if we want to create the most positive changes in our increasingly interconnected world.

I do not consider any faith as greater or lesser than any other. For me, there is an underlying goodness in our many different religions, and it may actually be beneficial that we do have different views within our many different faiths. All religions have their place in this world, with origins that were drawn from some sound principles and practices. Yet, no religion is perfect, no belief is absolute, and no person within these institutions are faultless. Is this not clearly the case with any religion when its people's hearts are full of anger, fear, and hate and it creates an atmosphere of arrogance, ignorance, and intolerance. Ultimately, this leads us into defying God's will which is peace, equality, and upholding the sanctity of each other's lives and then maintaining these as our personal foundation. Yet, this is the one thing our societies and religions have failed to resolve over and over again throughout history. I hope that more people will begin to see the bigger picture that is just beyond the narrow scope of their current viewpoint.

Where there is love, there is hope, and there is light. Where there is anger, fear, and hate, there is arrogance, ignorance, and intolerance and there is darkness. Anger and fear may be an instinctive reaction to stress, but we have the ability to turn them into choices. When we do not let go of our anger and fear it can push us into making poor decisions. Reactions filled with anger, fear, or hate are far more likely to end badly for all involved. Action fortified with a measure of calm that keeps your thoughts clear is much more likely to lead to better outcomes or everyone. And, if we have regrets in life, and we all certainly do, we should remember that they are but bookmarks, reminding us to approach those similar but new and challenging chapters in our lives, in a more thoughtful and conscientious way.

Torn: The Tear in the Fabric of My Soul

Restless Wind

Playfully, a slight waft of air tickles the calm water. It giggles softly as ripples spread out in all directions across its surface.

Swirling upwards then down the valleys, puffs of a breeze reach out and caress the trees. Vibrating needles hum as the pines softly murmur their gratitude.

Running headlong, the wind rushes up the mountainside. The snow jumps and flips, happy to perform acrobatic feats over the peaks.

Whistling, a rush of air sweeps low to the earth then rises up again. The trees bend and sway as the tall grass dances spellbound in the wind.

Spinning, a whirlwind takes form, jostling everything as it skips across the ground. Grumbling, the kicked-up dust reveals the earth's contempt.

On a giant draft of heat, the air streams up and over the mountains. The great granite monoliths sigh as it rushes by, wishing they could fly.

Out across the desert the restless wind wanders, sifting through the grit. The hot lethargic sand does not resist and allows itself to be shaped into shifting works of art.

The Simplest of Truths

Angry and thirsty, a hot mass of air moves out over the ocean. The water feeling the burn of the wind's distress, allows the parched air to drink deeply.

Racing across the vast sea a gale runs full force upon the water. The ocean swells up angrily in protest only to crest and crash wildly upon the shore.

Lazily, the light breeze drifts over the forest, breathing in moisture and exhaling rain. The jungle below reaches out and gratefully accepts the gift, letting the excess run to the sea.

Playfully, a slight waft of air tickles the calm water. It giggles softly as ripples spread out in all directions across its surface.

Who am I? Apart from what you have previously read about how I view my spirituality, I am married and have two children. My youngest is a child with special needs—she has been diagnosed with Rett syndrome. My wife and I have known this for quite a while now and have learned to cope with the day-to-day challenges. She does not walk or talk, but we feel fortunate that she has some use of her left hand. This is not the case with most Rett girls.

I love both of my kids without question. With my daughter, I know that I will shoulder any burden with her that I can, and I am very proud of how my son is growing up. He has an old soul for someone so young. That is likely a result of the unusual demands within our special-needs family. But, there are those days when I can look into my daughter's eyes and see the bright, intelligent mind trapped within; on other days, however, I can see and sense her sadness, and I know at these times there is nothing I can give her except a long hug and my love. We enjoy the good days and know we can make it through the bad days, but as for me, if I stop and dwell on things too long, I am overwhelmed by a powerful sense that there is a tear in the very fabric of my soul. I know with all clarity and certainty that my life is centered in the peace that is God, and I can draw strength from that, but I am not sure that one part of me will ever heal.

I struggle with the loss of potential my daughter was born with, or maybe it is just my expectation of what she should have had. Every day, part of me still mourns my daughter lost potential, and I live heartbroken knowing that Rett will eventually take her life. When accepting her for who she is, do I also have to concede that she will never be anything more than this? Where do you find hope, or how do you hold on to what little is left when the odds are insurmountable? I often ask myself, Is hope nothing more than a bright star in the darkening sky with no way of drawing nearer to it? Is my only option to accept things for what they are and know that, in the greater scheme of life, my daughter is who she is for a reason? At the end of each day, I resign to the fact that there are no answers I can accept, especially when measured against the potential value of even one life. Living tells me there is so very little to hope for, though my heart aches for it. And somewhere, down in the deepest part of me, I feel that God is telling me not to struggle, but I remain torn, and the restless wind blows through my soul.

The one thing I have come to understand is that the real power of love is in never giving up, especially on those who face the most profound challenges in life. Sometimes hope only amounts to nothing more than a small bit of light, but no matter how dim, if you allow it to, it can save you from the perils of an overwhelmingly dark path.

Sometimes God does not merely answer or grant prayers but will often open up possibilities or create opportunities. Maybe God cannot answer your prayers in the way you want them to be answered, but maybe God is already lifting you up or lessening your burdens in other ways. Be thankful for the things in your life that are going well, and do not shy away from life's challenges, for in them may be opportunities that move you closer to what you are praying for.

Murmurings

The diagrams on the front and back covers are not meant to try to connect emotions or God to science or physics. Instead, they are intended to show similarities in different spheres of influence.

Of Love-Earth-Gravity: by earth, I am implying its ecosphere; these three are about synergy, interactions, and relationships.

Of Anger-Air-Motion: this encompasses continuous change or the state of flux; these three are about the volatility of movement.

Of Fear-Water-Mass: by water, I am implying the weight rather than fluidity; these three are about heaviness and density.

Of Hate-Fire-Energy: this encompasses more than actions and reactions; these three are about residuals and the repercussions in turbulence.

What is pictured is nothing more than the creative outline for a line of thought: an observation of resemblances.

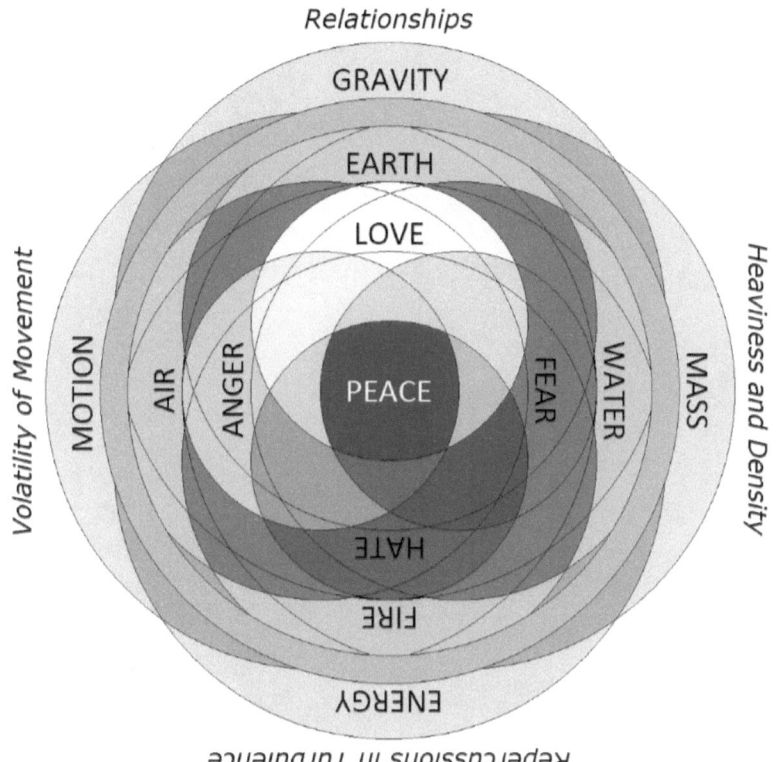

www.ingramcontent.com/pod-product-compliance
Lightning Source LLC
Chambersburg PA
CBHW020411080526
44584CB00014B/1269